HISTORY OF CALIFORNIA

The Lone Woman of Island of the Blue Dolphins

Travis "T.J." Frank

CONTENTS

ACKNOWLEDGEMENTS

" There must have been two dozen of them standing against the wall. They were as tall as I, with long arms and legs and short bodies made of reeds and clothed in gull feathers. Each one had eyes fashioned of round or obolong disks of abalone shell, but the rest of their faces were blank. The eyes glittered down at me, moved as the light on the water moved and was reflected upon them. They were more alive than the eyes of those who live."

- ISLAND OF THE BLUE DOLPHINS (CHAPTER 20)

Before we dive into the extraordinary life of the Lone Woman of San Nicolas Island, I wanted to acknowledge the men and women of the National Park Service (NPS) who worked tirelessly to bring the history of a forgotten people and a *Female Crusoe* back to the Californian consciousness. Thank you, for without you, not only would we- as Californians, Americans, and Californian Indians- have forgotten an important piece of our history but this book would not have been possible.

INTRODUCTION

"ISLAND OF THE BLUE DOLPHINS BEGAN IN
ANGER; ANGER AT THE HUNTERS WHO INVADE THE
MOUNTAINS WHERE I LIVE AND WHO SLAUGHTER
EVERYTHING THAT CREEPS OR WALKS OR FLIES."

- SCOTT O'DELL

Los Angles, California, 1959. In an archaic library, lies a table stacked with books, newspaper articles, maps, and records on California history and American Indians. A wise man hunches over the table methodically scanning through the open texts looking for someone. He had been in the library for weeks trying to locate any information on a ghost like figure who once stalked a small, deserted archipelago island in the early to mid-1800s. However, whenever he got close to capturing the ghost, at the last minute, the phantasm slips right through his fingertips. It seemed the phantom did not want to make its presence known.

Despite setback after setback, it did not stop author Scott O'Dell from finding the truth about California's very own *Robinson Crusoe*. Born on Terminal Island in Los Angeles, California, on the 23rd of May 1898, O'Dell Gabriel Scott had a strong connection with the natural world. Although Los Angeles is a bustling metropolitan today, back in the early 20th century, Los Angeles was rural, undefined, and wild. Growing up in rural Los Angeles, O'Dell spent many hours exploring beaches, learning about the plants and marine life of the Pacific Ocean.

While not exploring, O'Dell transported himself into books and became an avid reader. However, O'Dell's time in Los Angeles was short-lived. His father, Bennett Mason Scott, worked in the railroad industry that caused the family to move to different locations around southern California- from Rattlesnake Island (Terminal Island), Long Beach, and San Pedro- yet the O'Dell family was always near the oceans. When his family lived near the Mexican border, O'Dell witnessed firsthand the cruelness humans can inflict on the natural world. He watched hunters hunt the local wildlife with no remorse to the atrocity they were committing.

This moment would leave a profound mark on O'Dell's life. During his stay in San Pedro, O'Dell and his friends would paddle out to a tiny island- on twelve-foot-long logs towed from Oregon- not too far from the mainland called *Dead Man's Island*. Every summer, O'Dell and his friends had many adventures on the island. As he explored the island, O'Dell developed a kinship with the marine life- treating them like loyal companions- and viewed the tiny rock as a secondary home.

While he stood at the farthest edge of the island, O'Dell- gazing out into the Pacific Ocean- could not help but feel a longing; a longing for something he did not understand. Later in life, O'Dell would revisit these tranquil feelings and happier times as inspiration for his stories.

When he graduated from Polytechnic High School (Long Beach) in 1916, America was fighting in World War I. Hearing the call to battle, O'Dell decided to join the army, but the war ended before he saw any combat. With the war over, the now discharged O'Dell set his sights for college. He began studying at four different universities: Stanford University, the University of Wisconsin, Occidental College in California, and the University of Rome yet, he dropped out of all four. Why did he drop out of college? Was he not bright?

From O'Dell's perspective, the subjects he studied did not have the same punch except for writing. When he was a boy, O'Dell was inspired by his love of reading and found the writing in the books he read fit his personality- after his parents told him he was related to famed British author Sir Walter Scott. By his early twenties, O'Dell decided to become a writer, however, before he could pursue his dream, he had to find a job to keep a roof over his head.

By the time of the roaring 1920s, O'Dell began his six-decade writing career not writing fantastical stories, but penning articles for the local newspapers. One day while typing, the typesetter accidentally transposed his name in reverse. O'Dell liked the change so much he legally changed his name to Scott O'Dell. Within three years, O'Dell's writings were getting published, and he was making good money; however, he was not content where he was at.

O'Dell dreamed for bigger things and felt his writing could go somewhere than in forgotten newspapers. Then, O'Dell saw black and white. Setting his eyes on the burgeoning silent film industry, the 25-year-old O'Dell moved back to Los Angeles. While in Los Angles, he found work writing silent films, critiquing movie scripts, and even taught a mail-order writing course. With his writing becoming more respectable amongst his peer, O'Dell felt a calling to write a book. At 25, O'Dell published his first novel called *Representative Photoplays Analyzed.* During his decade stay in Hollywood, O'Dell would work different jobs at two major film studios: Paramount and Metro-Goldwyn-Mayer (MGM).

At Paramount, O'Dell worked as a set dresser and stood in for actor Rudolf Valentino-albeit his hands- in the silent film *Son of the Sheik.* At MGM, he worked as a cameraman and shot scenes for the biblical movie *Ben-Hur.* Despite the workload and good pay, O'Dell still made time for writing. It was during these formidable years scriptwriting, and working on movie sets, ignited O'Dell's passion for storytelling.

He enjoyed the process of writing stories for the silver screen that captured the imaginations of moviegoers of days gone by; and wanted to be part of the action. In 1934, he wrote his first novel, *Woman of Spain: A Story of California*. That same year, *Woman of Spain* caught the attention of actress Greta Garbo-who loved the story- and had MGM bought the film rights to the book but would never see production; though the sales would help him stay afloat during the Great Depression (1929-1945).

When World War II (1939-1945) broke out, O'Dell felt the war drum banging and joined the Coast Guard Auxiliary. He worked long nights patrolling off the coast of Southern California and would never seeing any action. After the war, O'Dell returned to writing full time. For his next novel, O'Dell wanted to write something he was passionate about.

Author Scott O'Dell

As a native Californian, O'Dell was obsessed with the state's long history and believed he could tell fanciful stories for an adult audience. It was after reading the history of the Mexican-American War (1845-1848), did O'Dell find inspiration for his next story. In 1947, O'Dell published his second novel, *Hills of the Hawk,* to critical success. Although he loved writing, O'Dell decided to take some time off from writing lengthy novels. He found work as a book editor for the Los Angeles Daily News but by the mid-1950s, he quit his position; as he felt the calling to writing again was too loud to ignore. O'Dell decided moving forward to work as a full-time author, but there was problem.

Although he enjoyed writing for adults, O'Dell ran into the same wall every writer slam into at least once in their career: writer's block. It also did not help that O'Dell- and his wife Dorsa- lived a busy social life, attending lavish parties and going out to expensive dinners with friends. O'Dell decided he needed to get away from his turbulent and loud social life and find somewhere that was quiet and near the ocean. He settled on the gold rush town of Julian, California.

Living next to the ocean again was a good welcome for O'Dell. While living in Julian, O'Dell became increasingly fascinated with the Indians of southern California. This new fascination became an inspiration for his next novel. In 1957, he wrote an informal guide called *Country of the Sun: Southern California and Informal Guide-* which includes an account of the 1870s Julian Gold Rush.

But it was during his research for *Country of the Sun* that O'Dell came across a folk story about a ghostly Indian who had lived on the isolated island of San Nicolas- off the coast of Santa Barbara- for 18 lonely years. O'Dell found the story so unbelievable he thought it was a work of fiction. Little did he know his life was about to change forever.

CHAPTER ONE

"Island of the Blue Dolphins," he wrote, "began in anger, anger at the hunters who invade the mountains where I live and who slaughter everything that creeps or walks or flies. So I wrote Island of the Blue Dolphins about a girl who kills animals and then learns reverence for all life."

- SCOTT O'DELL (PSYCHOLOGY TODAY JANUARY 1968)

Inspired by this mysterious Indian, in 1959, O'Dell began his research to find more information about this wild *Lone Woman*. During his research, O'Dell discovered an 1835 fall report from Charles Hubbard- captain of the schooner *Peor es Nada*. According to his report, the padres of Mission Santa Barbara commissioned Hubbard to go to the remote island of San Nicolas and bring back a small group of Californian Indians called the Nicoleño, safely back to the mainland.

What caught O'Dell's attention the most was Hubbard's description of a chaotic scene in which a Nicoleño woman was causing a commotion on the deck of the *Peor es Nada*. After boarding the gigantic schooner, the Lone Woman realized her baby was not on board with her and forgot him. In her madness, she began having a meltdown and vigorously tried to get back to the island to find her child.

Many attempts were made by other Nicoleño to restrain her failed when she managed to break free and leaped off the schooner into the murkiness of the Pacific Ocean. When she submerged, the Lone Woman had no time to look back and hastily swam back to the island to find her baby. As the schooner vanished from view, it would be the last time the Lone Woman saw her people. O'Dell became hooked and wondered why he was not aware of this moment in history.

Drawing of the Lone Woman w/dog

By 1960, the story of the Lone Woman was pretty much forgotten amongst Californians; who treated the story nothing more as Californian folklore. Even historians in the 1940s questioned if the story of the Lone Woman was true. However, O'Dell hoped to find more information and prove there was more to this story.

He decided to dive back into the dusty archives again. While scanning through the archives, something caught O'Dell's eye: two first-hand accounts of the rescuing of the Lone Woman by two otter hunters named Carl Dittman and George Nidever. In *The Life and Adventures of George Nidever* and Carl Ditmman's *Narrative of A Seafaring Life on The Coast of California,* Nidever and Dittman were tasked in the summer of 1853-by the padres of Mission Santa Barbara-to rescue the Lone Woman from loneliness and bring her to the mainland for her safety. Shortly after their arrival, Dittman and Nidever discovered the Lone Woman alive, in a crude makeshift windbreak made from discarded whale-rib bones. As she stood to greet them, Captain Nidever was stunned by her brightly colored strapped dress made from teal cormorant feathers.

> *"Her head, which had evidently been for years without any protection, was covered with thick matted hair, that was once black, no doubt, but now it had become of a dull brown color. Her clothing consisted of but a single garment of the skins of the shag [cormorant], made in the form of a gown. It fitted close at the neck, had no sleeves, was girded at the waist with a sinew cord, and reached nearly to the feet."*

This moment left an idyllic first impression on Nidever and Dittman. By the time her feet touched Santa Barbara in October 1853, the Lone Woman's life became headline news all over California:

> *"The wild woman who was found on the island of San Nicolas about 70 miles from the coast, west of Santa Barbara, is now at the latter place and is looked upon as a curiosity. It is stated she has been some 18 to 20 years alone on the island. She existed on shellfish and the fat of the seal and dressed in the skins and feathers of wild ducks, which she sewed together with sinews of the seal. She cannot speak any known language, is good-looking and about middle age. She seems to be contented in her new home among the good people of Santa Barbara."*

In her short time in Santa Barbara, the Lone Woman could not communicate with anyone. The only way she could communicate was through pantomime and symbolic gestures. Nidever learned how wild dogs on San Nicolas Island had eaten her son! Attempts were made to communicate with the Lone Woman but ended in repeated failure.

Whatever secrets she wanted to share with the world would remain as they were, secrets. Several weeks after arriving in Santa Barbara, the Lone Woman unexpectedly died. On her death bed, she was baptized and given a new name: *Juana Maria*. Not long after her death, her story faded into the background as an obscure California legend. In all his years of writing, O'Dell never felt a strong connection to a story; however, during his research, hunters were killing local wildlife near his Julian homestead.

This desecration deeply angered O'Dell. He considered writing a scathing letter to the local newspapers yet changed his mind-believing the press would not take his word seriously. O'Dell was still passionate about the natural world and wanted to get his message across to people of its importance. He looked back to the Lone Woman's story and had an idea. O'Dell realized the story of the Lone Woman could help him convey his passion for the natural world to the reader.

Island Of The Blue Dolphins

By late 1959, O'Dell began plotting a rough draft of his most ambitious book yet. He decided to take the historical account of the life of the Lone Woman on San Nicolas Island and tell it through a fictional lens but there were complications. O'Dell realized the story he wanted to write about was going to be great, but early on realized the story would be less appealing to an adult audience. He needed to make some drastic changes. O'Dell looked back to his boyhood adventures on *Dead Man's Island* and decided to make the Lone Woman's story not a retelling but a thrilling adventure story.

Island of the Blue Dolphins (1960)

One of the first changes O'Dell made was the age of the Lone Woman. From what he could gander from Nidever's account, the Lone Woman was in her 50s. O'Dell decided to dial the fictional Lone Woman's age to 12 years old. Why does this change matter? By making her age 12, O'Dell could tell the entirety of the Lone Woman's 18-years alone on San Nicolas Island. But more importantly, O'Dell wanted the reader go on a spiritual journey with her throughout the story; as a companion watching her become more self-reliant and grow up in a world that is unfair, yet still beautiful.

By the end of the story, the reader would meet the adult Lone Woman. As for the name of his main protagonist, O'Dell had to come up with a name that would be recognizable to a mainstream audience. He decided to call his protagonist *Karana*.

> *"Thus I was known as Won-a-pa-lei-, which means 'The Girl with the Long Black Hair,' though my secret name is Karana."*

For the Lone Woman's child, O'Dell changed the Lone Woman's

child to Karana's little 6-year-old brother. He named him *Ramo*.

> *"My brother Ramo was only a little boy half my age, which*
> *was twelve. He was small for one who had lived so many*
> *sins and moons, but quick as a cricket."*

He even went as far as making the remote San Nicolas Island into a living character. He wanted deserted island to be a watchful guardian to Karana until she was old enough to take care of herself. O'Dell transformed the ghost-like San Nicolas to an island that resembled a dolphin on its side.

> *"Our island...if you were standing on one of the hills that*
> *rises in the middle of it, you would think that it looked like*
> *a fish. Like a dolphin lying on its side, with its tail pointing*
> *toward the sunrise, its nose pointing to the sunset, and its*
> *fins making reefs and rocky ledges along the shore."*

Finally, he had to create a title that would be instantly recognizable. Reminiscing his early days exploring beaches, O'Dell decided to call this novel *Island of the Blue Dolphins*. O'Dell went to work creating a fantastical world that felt so real it would make the reader believe it happened.

To O'Dell, *Island of the Blue Dolphins* would become a personal story. Weaving historical events and love for the natural world, O'Dell hoped *Island of the Blue Dolphins*- a fictional, but historical biography of the Lone Woman- but would shed light on the story of a forgotten people, a remarkable Lone Woman, and the importance of the natural world. Overall, O'Dell's main intention was for the reader to walk away with the book's main themes of reverence for all life, and the ideals of forgiveness.

Worldwide Phenomenon

In less than a year, O'Dell completed *Island of the Blue Dolphins* in early 1960. Upon its completion, O'Dell showed it to his friends and literary agent and asked for their feedback. At first, they thought it was another historical novel for adults but became enthralled by the story, Karana, and her spiritual journey of self-reliance, determination, and survival. By the end, they felt like they were on an adventure with Karana on the *Island of the Blue Dolphins* themselves! Everybody agreed that this story was a powerful book not for adults but for children.

Having not considered this possibility, O'Dell took their advice and sent *Island of the Blue Dolphins* for publication for children. In 1960, *Island of the Blue Dolphins* splashed its way onto shelves and became a triumphant success amongst children AND adults; with parents praising Karana as a strong role model for girls all over the world.

Overnight, the Lone Woman's story went from being a California folk tale to a worldwide phenomenon. Even the critics found *Island of the Blue Dolphins* to be a literary masterpiece in children's literature. "*The girl, Karana, is portrayed in such intimate and close relationship with the natural elements of her background, the earth, the sea, the animals, the fish, that the reader is given both the terror and beauty of life itself. It is a book to make the reader wonder.*" Island of the Blue Dolphins would go on to sell over 6.5 million copies worldwide and be translated into 28 languages.

The following year, *Island of the Blue Dolphins* won the *Newberry Award* for children's literature. On the 3rd of July 1964, Universal Pictures released the film adaptation of *Island of the Blue Dolphins* starring Celia Kyle- who won a Golden Globe for new starlet of the year- as the titular Karana. Now audience members could join Karana's adventure on the silver screen. As of today, there has not been a re-release of the film nor new adaptations, but maybe one day the story could be fully adapted as a movie or made into a limited series.

Although *Island of the Blue Dolphins* is a work of fiction, teachers to fell in love with the story's themes as great teaching lessons for kids. To the teachers, *Island of the Blue Dolphins* helps kids get into and fall in love with American Indian culture and history. Today, the novel continues to be taught in elementary schools in California.

Actress Celia Kyle

The success of *Island of the Blue Dolphins* sparked a renewed interest of the Nicoleño and the Lone Woman's story amongst historians, Indian scholars, and archaeologists. Now, in the five decades since *Island of the Blue Dolphins* was first published, can the real story of the Lone Woman and the Nicoleño finally be told.

CHAPTER TWO

"Whether someone did stand there on the low hills in the days when the earth was new, and because of its shape, called it the Island of the Blue Dolphins, I do not know. Many dolphins live in our seas and it may be from them that the name came. But one way or another, this is what the island is called."

- ISLAND OF THE BLUE DOLPHINS (CHAPTER TWO)

For ten thousand years, Nicoleño fishermen has fished the blue waters of the Pacific Ocean. Every day, these brave seafarers rowed across a shark-infested ocean to find the best spot to fish. The Nicoleño would become known for their proficient skills as fishermen, who could handle the primordial winds and rains. Most experts agree the Nicoleño were given their name by the Spaniards- due to their similarities with southern Californian tribes like the Gabrielino, and the Luiseno- and centuries later in Alfred L. Krober's book *Handbook of Indians of California*.

The original name of the Nicoleño remains lost to history. However, many modern Californians are unaware there were Indians like the Nicoleño living on islands not too far from the mainland.If you were to look for San Nicolas Island on a map today, many Californians would not even know it was there. San Nicolas Island looked like breadcrumbs on a map than an actual island! At only 61 miles off the coast of the *San Pedro Channel*, San Nicolas Island is considered the most isolated island out of the Channel Islands. But what are the Channel Islands?

Located off the coast of California, there are eight archipelago islands divided into two channels: 4 in Santa Barbara (North)

Channel and 4 in San Pedro (South) Channel. Formed 5 million years ago, the eight Channel Islands rose from the primordial oceans- through tectonic forces pushing landmass from the oceans. As millions of years passed, each island developed unique plants and animals not indigenous to the California mainland. On the *Santa Barbara Channel*, lies the islands of *San Miguel, Santa Rosa, Anacapa, and Santa Cruz.*

Aerial view of the Island of San Nicolas

They are known as the Northern Channel Islands- where the Chumash made homes, influenced, and lived on for thousands of years. Further south on the *San Pedro Channel*, were the islands of *Santa Barbara, Santa Catalina, San Clemente, and San Nicolas.* These islands were under the influence of the Gabrielino. In terms of its topography, San Nicolas had a semi-arid climate where the winters were rare, the summers warm and dry- with February being the coolest time of the year. With these suitable conditions, it's no wonder the ancestors of the Nicoleño made the long trek to colonize San Nicolas Island. But how did the Nicoleño end up on San Nicolas in the first place?

Nicoleño Origins

Although isolated from their mainland counterparts, experts believe the Nicoleño were not originally from San Nicolas Island. Instead, most historians agree they were the descendants of ancient sea farers from the Californian mainland. Ancestors to all American Indians were descendants of ancient Asians who migrated across a land bridge connecting Russia and Alaska called the Bering Strait. From their arrival to North America, these early people colonized North, Central, the Caribbean, and Southern America.

Many migrated further south to their new homeland: California. As centuries passed, tribes began to form their languages and customs based on their location. Eventually, the the ancient Nicoleño found their new home along the rich Californian coastline. For the next thousand years, the ancient Nicoleño centered their culture on the coastline- learning how to use the ocean to their advantage. They built sturdy canoes called *ti'at* that took them out to sea. Over time, they became prodigious sailors able to sail up and down California with relative ease. Then, around 10,000 years ago, the Nicoleño felt boxed into the coastline.

They decided to sail further and further away from their homes to what would one day become San Nicolas Island. With no other people to compete for resources, the now indigenous people of San Nicolas could live freely, establish villages, and live off the island's coastline. Across generations, the Nicoleño enjoyed a prosperous and productive life on land and sea.

Passing Island

By the 16th century, the Nicoleño had lived unabated from the rest of the world. However, the ways of life Californian Indians enjoyed for generations was about to change. In 1521, Spanish conquistador Hernán Cortés conquered the fabled Aztec empire- opening Mexico to the power-hungry Spanish Empire. For the next ten years, the Spanish, bit by bit, explored and colonized all New Spain (Mexico). During one exploration in the mid-1530s, Cortés stumbled upon an unknown peninsula.

The Spanish Crown believed this peninsula was an untamed island untouched by the 16th century. They decided to call the island California- named after the mythical paradise island of Califia from a 1510 Spanish romance story *Las Serges de Esplandian* by Garcia Ordonez de Montalvo. The site Cortés discovered was Baja California. In 1542, the Spanish Crown wanted to find a quicker way to get to the West Indies and China. They did not want to make the lengthy journeys from Spain to the West Indies to get spices. The Spanish Crown believed there had to be a mystical river in the New World that could cut travel in half.

Under New Spain's viceroy, Antonio de Mendoza, commissioned Portuguese explorer Juan Rodriguez Cabrillo to find the mythical river-that would join both the Atlantic and the Pacific Oceans together- called the *Straits of Anian*. Mendoza also tasked Cabrillo to explore land claimed by Cortez to see if there were any rich cities for the Spanish to plunder and find suitable harbors for their ships to rest. Six days into his exploration, Cabrillo explored the wonders of California. He sailed up from Baja California up to Alta California (upper) and became the first European to enter San Diego Bay.

Any land he saw, Cabrillo claimed for the Spanish Crown. He even came into contact with the Indians- who sailed up to his ship offering them food. While sailing the uncharted California coast, Cabrillo visited the Southern Channel Islands except for one. While leaving the island of Santa Cruz in 1542, one of Cabrillo's pilots, a man named Ferrelo, sighted the tiny biscuit San Nicolas.

However, Cabrillo made no attempts to visit the island. From his perspective, San Nicolas was too small to have anything worthy of a value to claim for the Spanish Crown. Cabrillo also did not want to take his schooner that far out into the Pacific; where the weather was unpredictable and a slight chance his schooner could get destroyed in a violent storm.

As he passed, Cabrillo mockingly nicknamed San Nicolas the *Passing Island*. Cabrillo would sail further up California and realized that their new territory was not an island but an entire landmass-teeming with Indians. However, he did not find any riches. While on San Miguel Island, Tongva warriors ambushed

Cabrillo and his men, resulting in Cabrillo breaking his shin bone-that became infected, then gangrenous-resulting in his death on January 3, 1543. Cabrillo died not. finding the *Straits of Anian*-nor discovering rich cities- but claimed all of California for the Spanish Crown for future exploration and colonization.

Saint Nicolas Island

Although Cabrillo failed to find the *Straits of Anian*, the Spanish Crown was thrilled to discover their California territory was bigger than they originally believed. To help map the coastline of California, Mendoza enlisted merchant captain Sebastian Vizcaino. Back in 1593, Vizcaino helped settle a dispute over pearl fishing in California that got him in good graces with the Spanish Crown.

Like his predecessor, Vizcaino was to find the *Straits of Anian* and collect detailed information about California's shorelines- for suitable stops to dock and make repairs- water depths and natural weather for possible explorations. On May 5, 1602, Vizcaino, alongside two other frigates, left New Spain for the California coastline. While traversing the California coastline, Vizcaino made detailed sketches of the Northern and Southern Channel Islands- and named all the islands of the Santa Barbara Channel.

Then, on December 6, 1602, as he was passing the Southern Channel, Vizcaino spotted the *Passing Island*. Feeling pity for the little island, Vizcaino decided to give the small rock a more dignified name: Saint Nicolas. In the 15th century, Saint Nicholas was popular amongst sailors. During a pilgrimage of Jerusalem, Nicholas had a foreboding feeling to return to Lycia.As the ship made its way to the middle of the Mediterranean, a violent gust slammed the mast to pieces. Making matters worse, the gust was accompanied by forty-foot-high herculean waves, tossed the ship like a rag doll.

The sailors begged Nicholas to pray not only their safety but for the storm to dissipate. After two days and two nights of intense prayer, the storm ceased, and the ship safely arrived at the city of Myra. Knowing his miracle on the Mediterranean Sea, future sailors adopted Nicholas as their patron saint- he is more recognizable to many children around the world as the gift-giving Santa Claus.

Even though Vizcaino gave San Nicolas its name, he never set foot on the island. He probably took one look at the island and believed it to be desolate and not worth the hassle to explore- and feared his ship would get caught up in a storm. Due to these conditions, the Spanish explored other Channel Islands and much of California for greener pasture.

For now, San Nicolas Island would remain untouched for the next three centuries. Despite no longer being with us, archaeologists, anthropologists, linguists, historians, marine biologists, and American Indian scholars have worked tirelessly to bring the story of the Nicoleño back to the public consciousness.

CHAPTER THREE

"I came to the mound where my ancestors had sometimes camped in the summer. I thought of them and of the happy times spent in my house on the headland, of my canoe lying unfinished beside the trail. I thought of many things, but stronger was the wish to be where people lived, to hear their voices and their laughter."

- ISLAND OF THE BLUE DOLPHINS (CHAPTER 29)

When historians began their journey to uncover the secrets of the Lone Woman and the Nicoleño, they hoped to understand their culture, who they were, and what ultimately caused their extinction. However, errors and exaggerations have sneaked their way into the historical narrative of the Lone Woman and the history of the Nicoleño. Many scholars have relied on secondary sources- which they deemed as factual- on the Lone Woman, but quickly changed their tunes when they heard Scott O'Dell used George Nidever and Carl Dittman's memoirs.

To this day, their accounts provided historians a glimpse of the Lone Woman's life- and a hint of the Nicoleño culture. Although *Island of the Blue Dolphins* recaptured the imagination of the Lone Woman amongst the historical community, historians began their exhaustive search to find out what happened to this once thriving California tribe.

This story of the Lone Woman and the Nicoleño would become one of history's greatest detective stories. However, historians were up to the challenge. Luckily for the historical community, the Nicoleño would help them along the way. How did the Nicoleño help future historians exactly? As the last bastion left

San Nicholas Island in October 1835, they unknowingly left behind much of their belongings on the island. With a storm fast approaching the island, the Nicoleño had to quickly pack the essentials to bring with them to the mainland.

Due to their sudden departure, they could not take everything to the mainland. As a result, the Nicoleño inadvertently preserved much of their culture on the island. If historians wanted to move forward in their investigation, they had to make the long trek to San Nicolas Island. By spending time on the island, experts, not only unlocked the secrets of the Nicoleño and the Lone Woman but a forgotten piece of Californian history. However, it is a race against time since erosion and exposure has destroyed a lot of archaeological sites.

How Old Was The Lone Woman?

One of the first piece's historians needed to solve early on was the age of the Lone Woman. According to *The Life and Adventures of George Nidever*, when Nidever met the Lone Woman- for the first time- in the summer of 1853, he describes her age at around 50 years old.

> *"The old woman was of medium height, but rather thick. She must have been about 50 years old, but she was still strong and active. Her face was pleasing, as she was continually smiling. Her teeth were entire but worn to the gums, the effect, no doubt, of eating the dried seal blubber."*

If we extrapolate her age, the Lone Woman was born in 1800 or 1803. For decades, historians have debated the correct year of the Lone Woman's birth. There are conflicting reports-secondary sources- that the Lone Woman was in her mid-50s when rescued; however, after much deliberation, experts agree with Nidever's description.

The Lone Woman was born in 1803. With her age confirmed,

historians, archaeologists, and Indian scholars traveled to San Nicolas Island to begin their painstaking journey to unravel the history of the Nicoleño and the life of the Lone Woman. This is what they have discovered.

The Nicoleño And The Natural World
Sometime in 1803, the Lone Woman was born to two Nicoleño parents. We will never know the name she was given to by her parents, if she had any siblings- or living grandparents- or was a chief's daughter. But what we do know is the people the Lone Woman was born into. Since the Nicoleño once lived on the mainland, when they settled on San Nicolas Island, they based their culture on the coast.

  Despite being the most remote island of the San Pedro Channel, San Nicolas was home to many rich resources for the Nicoleño to live off for centuries. The sea surrounding the island provided much of their main diet. Many marine biologists have noted that San Nicolas is the only archipelago island to have rich deep kelp forests. These kelp forests provided comfort and safety for many fish and marine animals of San Nicolas. Within these dense forests, Nicoleño hunters killed Californian sheepshead, lingcod, Garibaldi, kelp bass, surfperch, and other types of rockfish. The Nicoleño also hunted marine invertebrates such as spiny lobster, crabs, and sea urchins, and even sea otters.

  When more experienced Nicoleño's went out fishing the sea, other hunters killed lizards, side-blotched, alligator, island night lizard, foxes, and mice. A staple diet of different kinds of fish, otters, and small invertebrates from the kelp forests ended up in Nicoleño cooking pots. When the men wanted to hunt for bigger game, they took their canoes and rowed further out into the Pacific. They hunted dolphins, sea lions, sea elephants, and even attempted hunting whales!

  However, the Nicoleño did not rely on the Pacific for food alone. The island itself- though small-provided them with different kinds of birds such as teal cormorants, seagulls, pelicans; and in special occasions, their eggs. While their diet consisted of rich fats and proteins, the Nicoleño needed essential vitamins and minerals to balance their marine diets. The only fruit on San Nicolas the Nicoleño coveted was the island's prickly pear cactus. These cacti contained delicious red-and juicy-fruits the Nicoleño loved to eat daily, but there was a problem.

To get their prize, the Nicoleño had to cut off the cacti' outer casing-coated with sharp quill-like spines. Whenever someone wanted to eat, the Nicoleño had to painstakingly remove the sharp spines first or get a mouthful of cuts! While mainland Indians had vegetables like beans, squash, pumpkins, potatoes, and corn as part of their diet, the Nicoleño did not have that same luxury.

Photo of the Lone Woman (1853)

There was only one vegetable the Nicoleño had grown to rely on for 10,000 years was a starchy bulb called blue dick corms- think of them as potatoes. To dig up the corms, Nicoleño gardeners used a special stick- with a round stone with a hole in the center-called the doughnut hole. The Nicoleño depended on the corms just as much as the ocean for their survival. Overtime, Nicoleño gardeners developed landscape management strategies to plant and harvest the corms. To keep the corms growing, experts believe the Nicoleño used controlled burning to encourage continual corm growth.

Each day, the gardeners tilled corm fields, harvesting mature corms, and planting baby cormlets. Once harvested, the Nicoleño would eat the corms cooked or raw. If eaten raw, the corms- acting like gum in your hair- would get stuck on their teeth! However, the Nicoleño would not mind the stickiness. Every day, a very young Lone Woman would've seen men out at sea trying their luck to catch bigger prey for their meals. She may have collected roots, seeds, de-spine fruits, and helped dig up corms for the tribe.

Abalone

While the Pacific provided much of their diet, there was one food the Nicoleño coveted above all else: abalone. Abalone are large marine snails- measuring at 12 inches- have small spiral design shells that could live up to 30 years. What made abalone special to the Nicoleño was the different varieties of abalone. Abalone came in colors: wavy brick red, smooth black, and vibrant pink. Because of their glossy reflective surface, the best spot to find abalone on San Nicolas was in deep water habitats- like the kelp forests.

Abalone served as a good source of protein for the Nicoleño's diet. Every day, the women would collect as many abalone as possible, pry open the shells, and leave the meat out in the sun- shrinking the meat. However, constant fishing in the 20th century reduced the abalone population. Today, there are many conservation efforts to save the endangered abalone from extinction, but during the time of the Nicoleño, they would have collected enough abalone to feed the small population.

Cooking

At first, you would think the Nicoleno ate all their food cold- based on their marine diet. However, the Nicoleño did cook their food. Cooking was primarily done by the women. For example, if the tribe wanted to eat the corms cooked, they constructed large earth ovens. Like the Luiseno, the Nicoleño's earth ovens were large pits dug into the ground where they placed their fires for cooking. After the fire burned down to coals, the cooks prepared the meal. The Nicoleño set the corms onto the coals and covered them with soil. This method allowed the heat and steam to remain locked in one place.

Once cooked, the server used a large abalone shell to scoop out the cook corms- that tasted like sweet potatoes - and distributed the food amongst other members of the tribe. It is likely the Nicoleño smoked and cooked most their fish, meat, and abalone because if uncooked, the tribe was in danger of ingesting viruses that could kill them. As a female, the Lone Woman would have learned how to cook and smoke food from her mother and other women within the village; so, one day she could take care of her husband, family, and the tribe.

Village

When the ancient Nicoleño decided to colonize San Nicolas, they had to find a spot close enough to the shoreline- not too far inland-and had a clear vantage point for incoming visitors or invaders. Archaeologists excavating the north coast of the island discovered the site of their village. They called the site *Tule Creek*. From the evidence, archaeologists learned the site was inhabited by the Nicoleño before their 1835 exodus.

Originally, *Tule Creek* went by a different name: *Ghalas-at.* For decades, the historians accepted *Ghalas-at* as the name given to the Nicoleño village, yet the Nicoleño did not call their village that name.*Ghalas-at* was the name given to the Nicoleño by the Chumash- who called San Nicolas *Haraashngna*- which Scott O'Dell then used for the name of Karana's village in *Island of the Blue Dolphins*. We may never know what the Nicoleno called their village.

The position of *Tule Creek* village was perfect for the small Nicoleño population. Its position overlooked the largest harbor on the island called the *Corral Harbor*- that allowed the Nicoleño a panoramic view of incoming ships and watching other members hunt at sea. *Tule Creek* was also close to a fresh spring for the tribe to drink. With these livable requirements, the Nicoleño was able to flourish.

Due to the size of the island, most experts believe *Tule Creek* had a population under 300-small enough to feed an entire village. They lived in small dome-shaped windbreaks and were 6 to 7 feet, had a small narrow opening on one side, slightly raised off the ground, and an opening on the roof to let out smoke from their fires.

Nicoleño Hut

What made the Nicoleño homes stand out from other tribes was the material they used from the ocean. Whenever the remains of whales washed up on the beach- and decayed under the blistering sun- the Nicoleño would take the whale's rib bones and tie them together using animal sinew or island grass as makeshift walls. The rib bones were sturdy enough to withstand wind- and from the wild dogs trying to sneak in to get free food.

Clothing And Body Decoration

Due to the Mediterranean like weather on San Nicolas, the Nicoleño were able to wear less clothing. Most experts believe their garments were made from cormorant feathers, duck skins, seal, fox, and otter furs. From Nidever's description of the Lone

Woman's dress, many experts speculate the women and girls on San Nicolas wore short to long strapped dresses; made from bird feathers and duck skins- by tying them together with a belt made from kelp. With the weather being warm on the island, the men and boys wore no top except for a loincloth. For decorative jewelry, the Nicoleño used discarded abalone shells to fashion together jewelry and beads. Both men and women wore jewelry and beads- either for decorative or symbols of status.

Arts And Crafts

The Nicoleño produced an array of material objects. Many of these items showed the uniqueness of Nicoleño artisans. For example, to store water, Nicoleño crafters created water bottles. They took island grass and weaved them together into the shape of a demijohn. From there, they took quantities of asphalt-found on San Nicolas- and set it in the bottom of the basket.

After the hot pebbles melted the asphalt, the Nicoleño coated the inside of the demijohn; which made the bottled demijohn watertight and light enough to carry. Another plant, found exclusively on San Nicolas, used by the weavers was the willow. The willow plants were used in the creation of willowed baskets- made from slender stalks of sandbar willow.

These willowed baskets allowed the Nicoleño weave together basket material to harvest abalones, clams, and shellfish. But there was one plant the Nicoleño used the most for crafting material was surf grass. Found too across San Nicolas, surf grass is a marine plant that appeared like long fine dyed green hair. The Nicoleño used surf grass to make home furniture such as living/sleeping mats. Surf grass also acted as a substitute rope to tie whale bones to the huts, securely fasten the roofs of their homes, and for cordage.

The women took strands of surf grass and twisted them until they became fishing lines to fish, nets to hunt and bags, and skirts for women.While not working on making hunting materials, Nicoleño crafters made special ornaments. These ornaments were crafted from a neat tool called a fused shale drill. The Nicoleño used Monterey Chert and the fused shale drills to create shell ornaments and beads-by using different seashells like red abalone, Olivella shell, California Mussel, clam, and Dentalium. For the broken abalone shells, the craftsmen would create bowls-by plugging their open holes with tar.

Tools

When archaeologists were scavenging the island for any tools the Nicoleño had left behind, they uncovered a rich cache of items that were still in the early stages of completion. They made Sedimentary Knives from Monterey and seco chert, Points Meta and Volcanic to hunt sea mammals around the island. Bones from pelicans, gulls, and cormorants provided raw materials to make bone tools.

To make their hunting tools, the Nicoleño used a variety of rocks- volcanic, lithics and steatite- to construct makeshift drills and whetstones; and a flaked piece of rock called biface, to sharpen both edges of their cutting tools. Whenever there were any leftover pieces of abalone shells used by craftsmen- to make ornaments and beads- the men would repurpose the broken pieces into digging/scooping tools. However, the most important tool to come out of these broken shells was the 'J-shaped' sharped edge fishing hooks.

These J-shaped fishing hooks were vital for Nicoleño fishermen. Without them, Nicoleño fishermen would not be able to fish-including deep sea fishing. To create the hooks, the men used a rock to carefully chip and ground abalone shells into the spiky J shape hook. You would find these J hooks in a Nicoleño fishing toolkit; made from redwood. Large abalone shells became lamps, dishes, and bowls- by sealing up the shell's open holes with asphalt- and even acted as shelves to hold their paints, food, and other resources. To entertain themselves, the Nicoleño constructed musical instruments using discarded bones from birds, mammals, and fish. These were called bone whistles.

Archaeologists digging around *Tule Creek* discovered sandstone saws the Nicoleño used to refine circular fishhooks. The Lone Woman would have seen men in the village working on making these tools and teaching their sons and other boys how to make them- and may have learned how to make them from her father or her future husband.

CHAPTER FOUR

"As I lay there I wondered what would happen to me if I went against the law of our tribe which forbade the making of weapons by women—if I did not think of it at all and made those things which I must have to protect myself."

- ISLAND OF THE BLUE DOLPHINS (CHAPTER NINE)

Back in chapter one, we discussed how Nidever could not understand the Lone Woman's language and consequently, we do not have a written first-hand account- from her perspective- of her life growing up on San Nicolas. Think of the Lone Woman's life as the picture on a jigsaw puzzle box. You take out all the pieces and get ready to put them together, but realize your missing half the pieces- i.e., the number of pieces the box promoted. That's how historians had felt when tackling the story of the Lone Woman: we only have pieces of the 1835 exodus, the 1853 rescue recalled by George Nidever and Carl Dittman, and her short time living in Santa Barbara.

Historians must speculate what daily life may have looked like for the Lone Woman. Growing up on San Nicolas Island at the beginning of the 19th century, the child Lone Woman would have played games with the other children on the beach, explored the tidepools, and swam in the ocean. While not playing with her friends, the young Lone Woman had daily duties she needed to complete before dusk: collecting roots, abalone, help tend the corm fields, prepare dinner- by skinning, de-boning, food captured for the day- alongside her mother, female family members, and other females of the tribe.

She learned how to use bone needles and surf grass to sew

together clothing made from fur, feathers, and duck skins. If she was not with her mother cooking, the Lone Woman spent time with her father observing how he made fishhooks, learned a thing or two about fishing, helped with hut construction (and repairs), and how he hunted cormorants and foxes- something she would come to rely on later in life. Every day, she had to work hard like everyone else to ensure the survival of their people. Little did she know their teachings would ensure her survival.

Language

As we know, after arriving in Santa Barbara in early October 1853, attempts were made to communicate with the Lone Woman. Linguists called on Indians in the vicinity to try and communicate with her, yet they too could not understand her language. This was a mystery for 170 years until modern experts uncovered a written record of the Nicoleño language. Apparently, those who were in contact with her were able to record only four words- *nache, toygwa, tocah, and puoo-chay*- she spoke, and a song she sang called the *Toki Toki Song*. But what do these four words mean?

Nicoleño	Possible Translation
nache	"man"
toygwa	"sky"
tocah	"hide" (skin)
puoo-chay	"body"

Modern linguists recently took these four words and compared them to other southern tribes. They discovered the four words had a closer relationship with languages spoken by the Luiseno, Tongva, the Cupeno, and the Cahuilla. This language was called *anapni'ts*. What is anapni'ts?

Anapni'ts was a unique form of *Uto-Aztecan* language spoken by the Gabrielino group- which includes the Fernandeno, Gabrielino (Tongva), and the Nicoleño -and since San Nicolas lies on the San Pedro Channel, the Nicoleño to spoke the same language; albeit a different iteration of anapni'ts. When it came to the *Toki Toki Song* was translated by an elder Chumash named Avario.

He claimed to have visited San Nicolas Island when he was a young man and interacted with the Nicoleño. From his short interactions with the Nicoleño, Avario picked up a little of their language. After hearing the song numerous times, he could translate the song. This is what the song said:

> *'I live contented, because I see the day when I want to get out of this island.'*

Why Avario did not speak with the Lone Woman remains a mystery. As we learn more about the Lone Woman, you will come to understand the connotations of the words.

Trade

Although San Nicolas Island was sixty miles away from the mainland, the Nicoleño traded with other Indians. How is that possible? Surely, they could have gotten lost on the high seas, drowned in a storm, or eaten by sharks? While impossible for many people to accept, trade between San Nicolas and the Californian mainland did happen. When pressed on the subject, Chumash elders claimed contact with the Nicoleño had been going on for thousands of years before Spanish Contact.

Through oral tradition, Chumash elders described the perils and danger their ancestors had to undertake to get to San Nicolas.Since crossing the channel was extremely dangerous and wrought with disaster, the Chumash used a specialized canoe called the *tomol*. The *tomol* used the best paddlers of the tribe- who were strong enough- to propel them from the mainland to

San Nicolas. But despite the dangers of the Pacific, these arduous journeys were worth it for both parties. Once a year, Chumash, the Tongva, and the Luiseno, traveled to San Nicolas to visit old friends, trade with each other, and find a suitable marriage partner.

Marriages between the Nicoleño and mainland Indians resulted in the exchange of gifts. For instance, if a Nicoleño married a mainland Chumash, Tongva, or Luiseno, they would move to the mainland or move to other islands- and vice versa. However, they can return home to visit their friends and families. To the Nicoleño, a connection between the island and mainland communities had to be strong because the bond allowed them access to items not found on the island.

Archaeologists digging up on San Nicolas confirmed this connection when they unearthed arrowheads and other tools from the mainland. Even shell beads from San Nicolas were found in southern California; reaffirming the bond. But if the Chumash and other southern tribes could make the trip to San Nicolas, then how did the Nicoleño travel to the California coastline without using a map? Many modern cartographers rely on compasses and maps to show where they were going while on the sea, yet the Nicoleño used the oldest map in human history: the stars.

At night, the seafaring Nicoleño used the constellations and star patterns as a map to get to the coastline. Historians are not sure what kind of canoe the Nicoleño used to get to the island- big or small- but whatever size they chose, the canoe had to be sturdy enough to get them to the mainland and back. However, relying on the stars alone as a map became a double edge sword for the Nicoleño. Weather changes can be unpredictable on the Pacific and if the channel happened to be foggy, the Nicoleño could not see the stars. As a result, they had to wait on the island until the fog had lifted-this also applied to forceful storms- yet this did not stop them from finding other means to travel.

Afterall, the Nicoleño had thousands of years of extensive

knowledge of wave patterns. While at sea, Nicoleño explorers could accurately predict waves coming in from the northwest would indicate they were close to the mainland- and figured out when it was safe or too dangerous to travel. We do not know what kind of canoe Nicoleño fishermen used to traverse to the mainland, but their canoes likely had to be sturdy enough- and large enough to carry goods and supplies- to make it to and back from the Californian coastline.

Warfare?

It's not known if the Nicoleño- in the 10,000 years they lived on San Nicolas- had fought wars with other tribes on the Channel Islands or were invaded from the mainland by other Californian Indians. However, scholars find this sketchy; since why would the already small Nicoleño tribe send their best men to fight for territory they couldn't maintain? San Nicolas had plenty of resources for them to live off from, so why leave an already small population even more defenseless? But as we will see, the Nicoleño did have the same tenacity for warfare.

Religion

After studying the Nicoleño culture for decades, experts claimed the religion they practiced was the *Chiningchinch* religion. What was the *Chiningchinch* religion? *Chiningchich* was the religious practice of making offerings and sacrifices. The Nicoleño would create large pits in the earth- not to be confused with their earth ovens- and place their offerings like beads, abalone, animal pendants, orch, seeds, and a bluestone called the Toshaawt stone.

During rainmaking ceremonies, the shaman used the Toshaawt stone to summon rain to help replenish fresh water on the island and help the blue dick corms to grow. We may never know what kind of god(s) they worshipped, yet it's highly likely the Nicoleño had a religious kinship with the natural world. Although not confirmed, the Nicoleño wore special animal pendants- made from soapstone- based on the marine life on the island. The most common was the *Mola Mola Pendent*. Experts believe these pendants connected the Nicoleño with nature and possible deities.

Dogs

The one animal on the island the Nicoleño coveted the most was their dogs. However, the wild dogs' readers are familiar with from *Island of the Blue Dolphins* were not originally indigenous to San Nicolas Island. Around 5-7,000 years ago, the Nicoleño brought over dogs-including foxes- from the mainland to San Nicolas. With no other predators on the island, the dogs, and foxes became the main carnivores. There were two different types of wild dogs you would have seen on the island: short noses with less fur and medium-to-large size-that resembled a coyote- with white or black fur.

Nicoleño hunters took their dogs out fishing, hunting animals, and served as warning guards when intruders were nearby. They even acted as pets and loyal companions. As archaeologists excavated graves near *Tule Creek*, they were shocked to discover these graves did not have Nicoleño in them, but their dogs. Whenever a dog died, the Nicoleño buried them in a special grave called *The Double Dog Burial*. *The Double Dog Burials* contained the remains of the Nicoleño's prized dogs and their possessions they had in life.

In the eyes of the Nicoleño, their dogs were their child and like any parent, wanted them to go to the next life knowing their masters loved them. Archaeologists later discovered a *Triple Dog Burial* that showed in one day, three dogs were put down for a ceremony or sacrifices. Since then, archaeologists have uncovered over 20 dog burials across the island.

Caves

One of the defining features found on San Nicolas is its caves. Some of these caves range from small to over one hundred feet long. While caves today may be fun to explore, to the Nicoleño, caves served as a place of shelter from harsh weather- when it got too hot in the summer, caves acted as a nice cooler- and became a secondary home for the tribe.

They would use caves as a suitable location to cook food, engage with others, make tools and art. The walls of the caves served as a blank canvas for Nicoleño artisans. When the Nicoleño first stepped onto San Nicolas, they used the island's caves to express themselves- through pictorial images- called rock art. But how did artists create images on the cave walls?

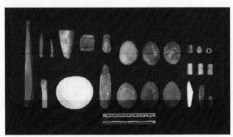

Nicoleño Artifacts

First, the artist used hand-held rocks to make the abstract representation of their world onto the rocky surfaces. From there, they painted the images using grounded powder, black charcoal, and red ochre. Some of these images are still on the walls today; however, the most famous cave on San Nicolas was called the *Cave of the Whales*. Located on the south end of San Nicolas Island, the *Cave of the Whales* depicts the beauty of marine life on San Nicolas; from the perspective of the Nicoleño.

They carved images of dolphins, fish, and whales, yet the Nicoleño did not use every cave for art. Some caves on San Nicolas Island acted as sacred religious sites -or holy ground- for worship. Because rock art is sacred to all American Indians, we must respect the past artisans and not tamper with them. The Lone Woman would have been fully aware of these caves and may have spent time exploring the caves when she was a child, but little did she know that her life, and the Nicoleño's, was about to change forever.

CHAPTER FIVE

"There will be none left. The hunters will kill them all. This morning they hunt on the south. Next week they move to another place."

- ISLAND OF THE BLUE DOLPHINS (CHAPTER THREE)

While the Nicoleño were enjoying their autonomy on San Nicolas, their mainland counterparts were enjoying a heavy dose of change. After leaving California alone for little over a century, Spanish monarch Carlos III became increasingly concerned about Russian and English exploration of the Pacific and stumbling upon the uncolonized territory. Between 1600 and 1750, the Spanish would occasionally visit the California coastline- as a pit stop between Mexico and the Philippines- but never occupied the region. That all changed in 1769, when Carlos III enacted the *Sacred Expedition* to "conquer" all of Alta California and its Indian population; however, he did not have the resources or the man power to launch an all-scale conquest.

Instead, Carlos III decided to form a friendship with the Indians. He issued *misiones* (missions) be built to help establish their new friendship with the Indians- while gradually converting them to Spanish citizens. From the eyes of the Spanish, a person can only be saved if they believe in Catholicism or was "civilized;" and since the Indians were still seen as uncivilized, it was the duty of the Spanish to save their souls from damnation.

The Spanish hoped their *neophyte* (baptized Indians) comrades-after spending years becoming a Spanish citizen- would be able to take care of themselves and own *doctrinas* (settlements). There, they would be given free land and have autonomy over it. The only way the mission system- and future colonies-could succeed in California if the Indians cooperated with the Spanish. Without the assistance of the Indians, there would be no missions or colonies.

The California Missions

To oversee the missions, the Spanish Crown enlisted priests from the Franciscan Order. The priests hoped the missions would provide a sanctuary for them to teach the Indians about God. However, their true goal was to combine the best features of Indian and European cultures. The Franciscans believed it was their sacred duty to save the Indians souls from damnation. From their perspective, the priests believed the Indians had to convert to Catholicism, adopt Spanish culture, appreciate manufactured goods as superior to their pagan goods, and forsake their traditional culture. However, the priests did not want to rush conversion onto the Indians.

They wanted them to continue living their traditional lives for ten years, but once those years were up, they would slowly introduce them to Catholicism and European customs. This kind of thinking is what ultimately doomed the Californian Indians. Under the leadership of Father Junipero Serra, walked up and down California called El *Camino Real (Kings Road)* finding missions- nine missions before his death in 1780-along the coast, planting elegant gardens, making aqueducts, and creating a spiritual kingdom in the West. But with progress came destruction.

Father Junipero Serra (1713-1784)

The life many California Indians enjoyed for thousands of years unabated came to an end. As new missions were founded, the priests gathered all the Indians in the surrounding area into one settlement called *reduccion*. This allowed the padres to organize all the Indians at once and made it easier for them to communicate. If the was no *reduccion* then the padres had to travel long distances to village after village teaching the Indians the same lessons, ceremonies, and religious rituals.

The priests- accompanied by soldiers- coerced many California Indians with new kinds of food, cattle, sheep, horses, chicken, mules, and steel weapons. Many neophytes were persuaded by the religious idolatry, music, and the spiritual teachings of the *padres* (priests) who promised them a "utopia;" where everyone would be treated fairly, and no one never had to go hungry- and could use them as allies against other Indians and European invaders.

Embracing Western religion, the neophytes returned to their villages to persuade their *gentile* brethren to join them. For a time, the gentiles ignored the Spanish call to the missions, however, as time went on, and more Spanish poured into California, they could no longer avoid the encroaching Spanish. Soon after, they joined the missions. From there, the neophytes helped build the missions, *presidios* (military forts), and convert to Christianity- with some secretly practicing their old religion.

However, once lured by the Spanish's false promises, the Indians were put to work. The padres taught them how to herd and raise cattle, make tools and goods- soap, candles, and horseshoes, and leather- and grow food; all they while increasing the mission's revenue. Overtime, the priests hoped the Indians would become experts growing food and not be dependent on hunting- destroying more of Indian culture.

What the Indians did not expect was having to work on a schedule. Every day, the mission bell rung across the vicinity indicating times to eat, prayer, work, and recreation. After eating breakfast, the neophytes went to work until the afternoon bell rung indicating lunch. They were given two hours to take *siestas* (naps) until the bell rung indicating dinner, than mass, then finally bed- where the men and women were separated and locked until the morning.

Indians plowing mission fields

As the missions expanded, the cattle, horses, sheep ate plants the Indians had grown and relied on for centuries-changing their diet overnight. Ultimately, the Spanish wanted the Indians- after spending 10 years in the missions- to be self-efficient and become tax paying Spanish citizens. While many embraced changes, others tried to maintain their traditional customs. Those who resisted or fled to their villages were shackled and imprisoned or periodically punished by the presidio soldiers.

Even the padres were in support of the punishment because

the missions depended on their exported goods and if they lose income, then the missions would shut down. Despite this cruelty, a majority became depended on the Spanish for their survival. To ensure the next generation of Indians not being taught of their traditional cultures, the padres indoctrinated neophyte children in Spanish culture.

This younger Indians raised in the missions- and Spanish ways- knew no life outside the church walls. The Nicoleño believed they would be unscathed; however, padres did take notice of other Indians on the Channel Islands- Santa Rosa, Santa Cruz, Santa Catalina, and San Miguel- and were successful in luring them off the island to the missions. It was only a matter of time before reality came knocking on the Nicoleño'a doorstep.

The California Fur Rush

Many Californians know the story of the *Gold Rush* (1848-1855). James W. Marshall accidentally discovered gold on his property in the Sierra Nevada, driving people mad with gold fever to make the dangerous trek across Indian Country and by sea to make their fortune in California. Many succeeded, many failed, but the sudden influx of people from different parts of the world helped create the basis of modern California. However, many Californians are unaware of another craze that predates the Gold Rush. Long before Marshall found gold, there was an international competition over an otter and its royal fur.

In the late 18th to the mid-19th century Russians, English, and Spanish were drawn to northern and central California; hunting foxes, raccoons, seals, weasels, beavers, and sea otters. These fur hunters skinned the animals of their precious fur and sold them on the international market for a ridiculous value. The fur hunters chose the San Francisco Bay Area as the center of the early fur trade in the west. Why San Francisco?

By making San Francisco Bay the center of the fur trade, traders could ship off their furs to regions where the demand was high. The fur trade helped open California and the Western Coast to the world. This moment in the state's history would become known as the *California Fur Rush* (1775-1840). The origins of California's endemic fur rush began by an accident in 1741. In 1741, Danish captain Vitus Jonassen Bering led a trading expedition east of Russia when his ship capsized on Russia's *Commander Islands*.

While shipwrecked, Bering and his crew found webbed footed sea otters propelling themselves through the waters. In desperation, the hunting party began hunting them in droves for survival. However, Bering made sure to preserve the otter's furs. Bering believed he could sell them to the open market to make up for anything of value lost, but Bering would not get the chance. On the 14th of December 1741, Bering died due to complications from scurvy.

Despite Bering's death, his crew was eventually rescued and brought 900 otter pelts to Russia. After selling the furs on the open market, the Russians discovered the bulk of their furs were bought by the Chinese. Otter pelts were highly prized in China because the sea otter has the densest furs of any mammal- on land or sea-and kept them warm in the winter.

After acquiring the furs, Chinese seamstresses went to work sewing together otter belts, capes, and clothes for the elite. The Chinse dubbed the otter pelts *royal furs*. These *royal furs* on the Chinese market sold anywhere between $80-100. In one day, the Bering expedition made $72,000-100,000!

Wanting to get into the possible fur craze, England threw their hat in the fur game. Between 1775 and 1777, the English killed and sold off 29,000 otter pelts to the Chinese market. In one day, the English made $300,000. Seeing an easy payday, the Spanish decided to get into the otter hunting game as well. They ordered the coastal natives to comb the coast for sea otters and seals for them. In exchange for their cooperation, the Spanish traded abalone shells, beads, metals.

Then in 1784, Spanish entrepreneur Senor Vincente Vasadre y

Vega became the first man to organize and expand the Western fur trade, by taking the otter pelts from the Indians, and shipped off to New Spain where otter pelts were cleaned, tanned, and sold off to China for quicksilver. By 1785, word officially got out of the rich value of the *royal* furs. The demand for *royal furs* was in full swing. The California Fur Rush had officially begun.

Sea Otter Pelt (Royal Furs)

During the early 19th century, the coast of California became a hot contention for international competition between the Russians, Spanish, English, French, and Americans broke out over who could capture the most otter pelts. From 1803 to 1805, approximately 17,000 otter pelts shipped from California to the international market for sale. Although the royal furs provided each nation with easy cash, they nearly cost the extinction of sea otters in the west. By the end of the 19th to the early 1900s, the number ballooned to 500,000 pelts! To this day, otter populations in the west are still recovering.

The Russians And Alaska

Although otter hunting became a prized commodity amongst Europeans, the Spanish, and Americans, they were amateurs in the eyes of the true masters of the hunt: the Russians. Before they sailed up and down the coast of California, the Russians did most of their hunting in the Northern Hemisphere. Regular sailors would not last a week in the sub-freezing temperature; however, the Russians were all too familiar with the unforgiving cold.

For generations, they learned to adapt and build a tolerance to the cold. Russia is known to have some of the harshest winters that required its people to wear fur clothing to keep warm; otherwise, many would freeze to death! Russian hunters hunted otters in the hundreds up and down the Northern coast of Vladivostok.

Thanks to advancements in caravel technology during the 18th century, the Russians could venture deeper into the heart of the Vladivostok coastline to hunt otters and seals. Then in 1741, the Russians set their eyes on Alaska's Aleutian Island chain- extending east from the Bering Sea and the Gulf of Alaska- as their new hunting grounds. The Aleutian Islands were home to a tribe of American Indians called the Aleutians (*Aleuts*); a people the Nicoleño would come to know personally.

Arriving on the islands, the Russians formed an alliance with the Aleuts so together, both parties could otter and seal- that populated the island's rocky coastlines. As time went on, the Russians set up a trading station- and a center for exporting otter pelts to China- where they traded with the Aleuts for furs and other commodities. Many Aleuts also benefited from this alliance with the Russians. In exchange for the furs they caught, the Aleuts received goods, metal tools, becoming Christians, etc.

Although this healthy alliance benefited both parties, it was about to come to a screeching stop when the otter population began to decline-done by overhunting. Each time the Aleut hunters returned from hunting, they brought with less fur; increasing the Russian's already growing frustration.

With the demand for *royal furs* in full swing, the Russians knew it was only a matter of time before other countries would overtake them as the number one exporter of *royal furs* in the world. The Russians became desperate. They forced the already exhausted Aleut hunters to venture into dangerous waters of the North Pacific to hunt for more otters. This uneasy alliance went on for a time until 1763. After receiving fewer goods for the furs, they collected, exhaustion and atrocities conducted by merchant captain Ivan Bechevin's men on Unimak Island, the Aleuts had enough and rebelled.

Despite being at a technological disadvantage, a combined Aleutian force managed to take down four Russian vessels. Bent on revenge, the Russians fought back. They stormed Aleut villages, destroying hunting gear, boats, murdering chiefs, and elders, and taking the women and children as hostages.

In those grueling months, the Russians violently abused their Aleut prisoners- as a warning to the Aleutian men who had the gall to fight back. Seeing no other option, the Aleutian men capitulated to the Russian's demands and surrendered. This moment in Aleut history would become a lasting scar. The autonomy the Aleuts have enjoyed for generations came to an end. In 1784, Empress Catherine the Great helped explorer Grigory Shelekhov's mission to set up a permanent residence in Alaska; and trade with the Tlingit people.

Women wearing sea otter garnments

However, in 1803, the Tlingit- like the Aleuts before them- rebelled against the Russians after their mistreatment and successfully destroyed several Russian settlements. After the

Battle of Sitka (1804), the Russians and all Alaskan natives signed a peace treaty that established a new status quo of peace.

From 1804-1867, the Russians and Alaskan natives-including the Aleuts- would hunt together and live amongst each other in peace. However, by the early 1800s, the otter population was nearly diminished in Alaska. Seeing their golden goose vanishing, the Russians left Alaska and headed south to California. There, they hoped the otter population was more plentiful.

The Russian American Company

As tensions for *royal furs* began picking up steam, the Russians needed to create colonies- outside of Alaska- on the North American coastline to quickly export furs to China. In 1781, Russian merchants Ivan I. Golikov and Grigory I. Shelikov came together to create the *Northeastern Company*. When Shelikov died in 1795, the company merged with three other Russian groups to form the *United American Company*.

However, by the dawn of the 19th century, the international competition for *royal furs* was out of control! The Russians needed to create a company that could confront foreign competition on the world market. In 1799, Tsar Paul I created a new monopoly- in which all other Russian companies merged- to form the *Russian American Company*. According to Paul I's decree, the *RAC* was granted a twenty-year charter that gave them exclusive trading rights in North America; however, with Alaskan otter and seal populations in steep decline, the Russians needed a new hot spot to hunt. Luckily for them, their dilemma was about to change.

In 1803, an American captain named Captain O'Cain stopped by the *RAC* headquarters and informed them about seeing large otter populations on the California coastline. Although this was a sign of good faith by O'Cain, he did not want the RAC to get all the profits. He agreed to take the Aleuts to California to hunt otter on the condition to split the profits 50-50; to which the *RAC* agreed to the terms. This was the answer the Russians needed, and it was only going to get better for the *RAC*.

Флагъ Россійской Американской Компаніи.

The Russian American Flag (RAC)

In 1810, New Spain had begun its fight for independence from Spain. This revolution had immediate effects on California. With the Spanish Crown preoccupied with squashing the rebellion, their officials could not enforce their strict trade restrictions in California; resulting in increased and unabated hunting and foreign trade in California. In 1812, the Russians, seizing the opportunity to capitalize on the chaos in New Spain, established two forts, *Bodega Bay*, and *Fort Ross*. *Bodega Bay* served as the center for Russian hunting, with *Fort Ross* serving as the main trading post.

In the years that followed, Russian ships began appearing off the coast of California. During their thirty-five-year reign, the *RAC* captured over 100,000 pelts in California. Around this time, the Americans got into the fur trading business. They decided to hunt and kill otters instead of trading with the Californian Indians. Despite making a trade alliance with the then Thirteen Colonies in 1763, the Russians saw American merchants and hunters as an intrusion over their domain. Tension arose amongst both nations that could have resulted in war!

However, after strict negotiations, the Russians and the Americans signed a truce and agreed on a joint coalition- hunting otter together for a time- in March 1812. While that was going on, Captain O'Cain led a hunting expedition into the Channel Islands and discovered larger otter populations on San Nicolas. In

1814, the *RAC* ordered Russian Captain Iakov Babin and 30. Aleut hunters to take the *Il'mena* to San Nicolas Island to hunt for otters. What happened next for the Nicoleño would change their lives for the worse.

The Nicoleño Massacre

By the early part of the 19th century, San Nicolas had become the prime target for frequent visitation. Due to its isolation, San Nicolas allowed the hunters to elude Spanish authorities and bypass their permission to hunt. It also helped that Spain was still dealing with the rebellion in New Spain and could not maintain its strict trade restrictions. Because the islands are off the coast of Spanish California, the Russians didn't have to worry about getting into conflict with the Spanish. In late 1814, Captain Babin and the Aleuts made anchorage near the eastern edge of *Tule Creek.*

The weather was nice and clear that day when the young Lone Woman caught a glimpse of their sails gliding towards the island. By 1814, the Lone Woman would have been around 11-12 years old. Seeing fair-skinned men and other Indians would've amazed her. What transpires next remains highly speculative amongst experts. After setting foot ashore, Captain Babin would have contacted the Nicoleño and asked their chief's permission to hunt otter on the island. In exchange for their cooperation, Babin promised the Nicoleño gifts- in beads.

But what started as an easy truce between the Nicoleño, Babin, and the 30 Aleuts, turned sour. For several months, the crew of the *RAC* and their Aleut hunters egregiously hunted otters all over San Nicolas. They hunted throughout the day-returning to camp at dusk- skinned otters all night, and by dawn, left the beaches coated with the blood of the otters.

Seeing this act of barbarism would not have gone unnoticed by the Nicoleño; they too rely on the otters for food and materials. If the Russians and Aleuts continued their onslaught on the island's otter population, there may not be any left for the Nicoleño! As you can imagine, the Nicoleño were not too happy. During their several-month carnage on the island, there was a breaking point between the Nicoleño and the Aleut hunters.

Many historians agree that an argument broke out between the Nicoleño and the Aleuts over the number of furs the Aleuts had accumulated- or over women-resulted in the murder of an Aleut hunter at the hands of the Nicoleño. Upon hearing one of their own murdered by the Nicoleño, the Aleuts demanded revenge. Babin, having no respect for Nicoleño sovereignty, allowed the Aleuts to quench their thirst for blood. The blade-wielding hunters stormed *Tule Creek* and murdered Nicoleño men and took some of their women as hostages.

The Nicoleño stood no chance against the better equipped and superior numbered Aleuts. The young Lone Woman would've bore witness to this deadly massacre by the Aleuts. We can only imagine if she was one of the taken- then released- or hid. Whatever happened to her at this moment may have shaken her and maybe traumatized her for years, but since she is not around to tell her part of the story, we will never know the truth. By the end of the massacre, there were barely any men- of hunting age-left. As for Babin, he did not care what happened to the Nicoleño. He got his *royal furs* and was contempt leaving the Nicoleño broken. The Nicoleño would never be the same again.

CHAPTER SIX

*"At that moment I walked across the deck and, though many
hands tried to hold me back, flung myself into the sea."*

- ISLAND OF THE BLUE DOLPHINS (CHAPTER 7)

Although Babin was responsible for the Nicoleño massacre, his actions didn't go unnoticed. When *RAC* officials heard word of the Nicoleño massacre, they were horrified. Three *RAC* managers, Ivan Kuskov, Leontii Hagemeister, and Semen Ianovskij, were enraged over Babin's irrational decision to allow their Aleut hunters to murder the Nicoleno; and disturbed by the large body count. The *RAC* wanted to forge an alliance with the Nicoleño, not to repeat past sins! By the end of their inquiry, all three officials convict Iakov Babin inhumane actions and as the instigator for the Nicoleño massacre.

Despite the main instigator for the massacre faced justice for his crimes, it was already too late. From 1814 to 1835, there were more visitations from hunting parties to San Nicolas Island, and this time they brought a new weapon: disease. With little to no immunity to European diseases, the already small Nicoleño population- whom historians argue may have been smaller before due to other Indian brining back diseases through trade- stood no chance.

To make matters worse, the once-thriving otter populations the Nicoleño relied on for subsistence and materials was in the early stages of decline; due to overhunting. The Nicoleño were now on borrowed time. In 1835, padres from Mission Santa Barbara caught word from returning hunting parties of the microscopic group left on San Nicolas. Fearing their extinction, the padres desperately wanted to save the remaining Nicoleño before it was too late-and seeing fresh new converts to exploit. The padres pleaded with German Captain Charles Hubbard to take his schooner, the *Peor es Nada* ("Better Than Nothing"), to San Nicolas to bring the weary Nicoleño to San Pedro to ensure their survival.

A Different California

While the Lone Woman languished alongside other Nicoleño on San Nicolas, California changed hands. After earning their independence from Spain in 1821, Mexico set their eyes on California. Under the Mexican government, Mexican officials wanted to give land- owned by wealthy missions- to *Californios*. To do this, the Mexican government had to secularize all 21 missions in California and take control away from the corrupt padres.

In return, the government would give mission land and livestock to the neophytes and Mexican citizens to make *ranchos* (ranches). The duty of the ranchos was for the *ranchero* (rancher) to oversee the household, produce wine, grow grain, and herd cattle. These new goods became the new backbone to California's economy- usurping the mission's more than five-decade control of California.

As for the neophytes, they were given small parcels- that was sadly once theirs- with the best going to wealthy rancheros, Californios, and Spanish descendants. Although a new government had come into power, Spanish policies remained intact. The neophytes- who did not receive any land- went from being enslaved in the missions to becoming serfs on the ranchos.

> *"The natives...in CA... are in a state of absolute vassalage (slavery), even more degrading, and more oppressive than that of our slaves in the south....It is quite certain, that the labors of Indians will, for many years be as little expensive*

to the farmers of that country, as slave labor."

Now on the ranchos, the Indians helped the rancheros herd cattle and livestock, brand, or slaughter all the while being paid nothing.

> *"The Indians...do all the had work, two or three being*
> *attached to the better house [wealthier rancheros]; and the*
> *poorest persons are able to keep one [Indian], at least for*
> *they have only to feed them and give them a small piece*
> *of coarse cloth and a belt, for the men, and a coarse gown,*
> *without shoes or stockings, for the women."*

What's worse for Californian Indians, if the ranchero was short on labor, he had other Californios raid villages and force them to a life of servitude. Those who gained free land grants from the Mexican government did not fair any better than the Indians on the ranchos.

The Old Spanish and Mexican Ranchos Map

Many were forced off their land by Californios; however, things were about to change in California in a big way. Back east, Americans had heard stories of life in California, the missions, the beautiful climate, the ranchos, and Spanish/Mexican culture, and the weak government. Many believe the Californios were lazy and weak because they did not fully utilize the potential of California's natural resources.

By the 1830's, Americans began the long trek to California, but the road to get there would not be easy. Those traveling by wagon had to cover 2,000 miles of endless land, boredom, exposure, travel through *Indian Country*- praying they did not get attacked by Indians- or die from disease or starvation, yet not everyone made it to California. However, those who made it to California refused to become Mexican citizens or convert to Catholicism. Why does this matter?

In accordance with Mexican doctrine, officials could only grant land to foreigners if they either convert to Catholicism or become a Mexican citizen.Since most Americans in the east were Protestant Christians, they refused to comply; with many settling in California illegally. The Mexican government could do nothing as California was slowly being infiltrated by Americans- something the Spanish were all too familiar with. The California the Nicoleño were going to was not the same California they had known for generations.

Moving Day
According to conflicting sources, the Nicoleño (pre-massacre) stood at around 300, but by 1835, the population dropped to 20 to 10 members- many experts believe the number was seven. By 1835, the Lone Woman was already in her early thirties.

> *"She was a widow, between, twenty and thirty years of age, of medium height, and fine form; her complexion was light, and her of a dark, rich brown."*

Having witnessed her people slain by the Aleuts two decades prior, more visitations, and seeing loved ones succumbing to diseases, may have left the Lone Woman traumatized and heartbroken. However, the Lone Woman did find joy in all the chaos.

She had met and married an unknown Nicoleño man and had a son- who we will never know his name- whom she loved dearly. Written accounts would later say that on moving day, she was single, yet experts believe her husband most likely died from disease or was one of the Nicoleño who left on the *Peor es Nada.* What comes next comes in the story of the Lone Woman comes from a firsthand account from American otter hunter Isaac Sparks. According to Sparks, in October 1835, the weather was dark and cloudy as the giant schooner landed on the eastern end of San Nicolas.

As they marched up to *Tule Creek*, Hubbard went to work to convince the remaining Nicoleño to leave the island. It is unclear if Hubbard had a translator for anapni'ts but whatever method he used to convince the Nicoleño seemed to work. The Nicoleño hastily began packing their belongings to bring to their new home in San Pedro. We can only imagine how they felt at that moment. Some probably did not want to leave their ancestral home, yet more levelheaded members believed it was best to leave the island and survive on the mainland with other Indians. But this rescue could have been an excuse to remove the Nicoleño off the island.

Removing them from the island meant future hunting parties no longer had to deal with hostility from the Nicoleño and could hunt to their heart's content. As the remaining Nicoleño boarded the Peor es Nada, the weather took a turn for the worse as a storm rocked the Pacific. Not wanting to get caught in the eye of the storm, the schooner had to leave now! But as they were getting ready to depart, there was a commotion on board. According to Sparks' account, he claimed the Lone Woman was frantically panicking her baby was not on board and realized-in the confusion of packing and moving- she accidentally left him sleeping in their hut.

*"In the excitement and confusion of the final
abandonment of their home, it was not known until they
were on the ship that a child had been left behind. The
mother supposed it to have been carried aboard in the arm
of an old sailor. She frantically implored the men to return.
The captain [Hubbard] replied that they must go to a place
of safety; after the storm tomorrow, perhaps—they could
come back for the baby. Finding that they were going out
to sea, the young mother became desperate, and despite
all efforts to detain her, jumped overboard and struck out
through the kelpy waters for the shore."*

After she plunged into the kelpy waters, Hubbard refused to
launch a small boat to pick up the castaways. With the storm's
unpredictable power on the ocean, Hubbard decided to leave them
for one week and return when the storm had abated.

*"No attempts was made to rescue her, and in a moment
she was lost in the seething waves. The ship, already under
headway, staggered through the storm; the affrighted
islanders huddled together on the deck, and fear shut every
other emotion for the time from their hearts."*

By the time she made it to shore, the white sails of the *Peor es Nada*
vanished into the storm. The Lone Woman was now alone. But
did this remarkable event really happen?

Did The Lone Woman Jump Ship?
Historians have debated if the Lone Woman had indeed jumped
off the schooner to find her missing child. They claim that
within their small group, there was no way the Lone Woman
could have forgotten her baby! Everyone would have known the
Lone Woman's baby and reminded her if she forgot him. It is
more likely the Lone Woman's child was not a baby, but a small
boy. More recently, there was a new a record from Isaac Sparks
detailing a completely different picture that day. *"Having got all*

the Indians together on the beach ready for embarking, one of them made sign, that her child had been left behind whereupon she was allowed to go back and fetch it."

According to this new account, the Lone Woman was not on the *Peor es Nada*. Therefore, she did not jump off the schooner and swam to the shore but went back to *Tule Creek* to look for her baby. This account, on paper, seems more plausible because it allowed the Lone Woman more time to get to the village, grab her baby, and make back to the beach. Many experts believe this moment in the Lone Woman's story had changed over time to the point of romanticism. There are two possible scenarios to what happened on that fateful day: on moving day, the Lone Woman had gone to the beach, but her little boy was not there.

Panicking, she made signs to the crew that her child was not with her and had to find him; which they allowed, but she had to act quickly because a strong gale sprung up.Now on borrowed time, the Lone Woman had to act fast and find her son. She looked everywhere- and around *Tule Creek*- for her boy until she discovered him hiding in the bushes; scared of captain Hubbard and his crew. With her son safe, the Lone Woman tried to persuade him to come with her to the beach, but he refused. She reassured him they were going to a better place, yet he refused again. He did not want to leave his home.

We may never know if the Lone Woman grabbed her son and dashed to the beach, only to discover the *Peor es Nada* had left without them. However, it is more likely the Lone Woman, not wanting to upset her child, made a painful decision: she would stay behind on the island and raise her son. Once she made her choice, she would never see any of her people again. As time went on, the gale was growing to dangerous levels.

Not too long after she left the group, a gale lashed across the shoal waters. Seeing the Lone Woman taking too long, Hubbard ordered his men to get the remaining Nicoleño onto the *Pero es Nada* and set sail for San Pedro. By the time the Lone Woman-with her son by her side- made it to the beach, the schooner was gone.

They were the last remaining Nicoleño on San Nicolas Island.The second scenario goes like the first, but instead of the Lone Woman looking for her son, its her baby. The Lone Woman goes off to *Tule Creek* to grab her baby- on borrowed time- but when she made back to her hut, the baby was gone. Knowing her baby was taken by the wild dogs, frantically went looking for him and found him dead.

As everyone waited for her return, the weather took a turn for the worse and Hubbard ordered his men to get the Nicoleño on board the schooner and set sail. He would not wait for her to return. As the schooner left San Nicolas, the Lone Woman would have made it back to the beach only to see everyone was gone. She was now alone. However, experts lean more towards the first scenario that the Lone Woman was not entirely alone but spent considerable amount of time living with her son.

CHAPTER SEVEN

"The huts looked like ghosts in the cold light. As we neared them, I heard a strange sound like that of running feet. I thought that it was a sound made by the wind, but when we came closer, I saw dozens of wild dogs scurrying around through the huts. They ran from us, snarling as they went."

- ISLAND OF THE BLUE DOLPHINS (CHAPTER 8)

After the *Peor es Nada* sailed away from San Nicolas for the final time, the traditional story of the Lone Woman ends here. All we have is a glimpse of the Lone Woman's life on the island thanks in part to Nidever's memoir and Emma Hardacre's 1880 historical account. Through both recollections, Nidever and Emma explains how the Lone Woman explained- using symbols and pantomime- what her life was like on the island for 18 years. Although she enjoyed living on the island with her son, the Lone Woman was sad. She was sad because she decided to stay behind with her son, while her people went ahead to a new and hopefully better life on the mainland.

Everyday she would look out to sea for the *Peor es Nada,* but when the schooner did not return, she would always tell herself manana (tomorrow). She had good days and bad days; however, it did not stop her from believing that someone - at the behest of her people-would come back to pick them up. In the meantime, she had to provide for her son and herself. The years of constant repetition of cooking, cleaning, collecting, etc., was about to pay off. Since the Lone Woman could not tell her side of the story, historians had to speculate what she did daily.

For instance, the pair had to find a suitable place to live. Believing the *Peor es Nada* would return, the Lone Woman and her son may have stayed at *Tule Creek* for a time. She wanted to be ready to go as soon as the schooner landed. As the days passed, the Lone Woman and her son explored every inch and crevice of their island. They visited the caves of their ancestors where she told him stories of heroes long gone, the natural world, and the importance the caves are to their people. Seeing how much room a cave could provide, the Lone Woman decided to make one of the caves their new home. She was going to thank this cave later.

While they waited, the Lone Woman had to become both the mother and father to her son. As the mother, the Lone Woman taught her son how to gather roots, abalone, dig up and maybe grow corms for their cooking pots. She would've taught her son how to use kelp and sinew to tie together whale bones to huts, mend and make clothing. Depending on the age, the Lone Woman's son may have had some experience in fishing, from his father. With the men in charge of big-scale hunting now gone, the Lone Woman had to improvise: by becoming a hunter. Fortunately, she had learned how to make durable tools- from observing the men, her father, and husband- to hunt small game.

Acting as the father, the Lone Woman taught her son how to hunt island foxes, gulls, fish, the teal feathered cormorants, and possibly otter. As for larger prey, she learned how to kill seals by catching them off guard while they slept by dropping a devasting stone on their heads! Daily, the Lone Woman would have instilled these lessons into her son because if she unexpectedly died, he needed to be able to provide for himself. Then on a cloudless day, she saw what appeared to be clouds on the water. But they weren't any clouds but sails from a schooner!

At last, the Lone Woman believed the *Peor es Nada* had returned to take them off the island; however, the ship didn't change direction and kept going until it was out of view. The Lone Woman was confused why the schooner did not come to the island. In her confusion, the Lone Woman became devastated and wept. As seasons went and years passed like a comet, the Lone Woman would see more ships pass by the island. Each time schooners sailed by San Nicolas Island, the Lone Woman despairingly wept, wished, and prayed that one of them would take them away from the island.

Female Crusoe

For a time, there was a prevailing myth that after the *Peor es Nada* left San Nicolas in 1835, the Lone Woman and her son were left alone for 18 years- visitations from hunting parties otter ceased due to the declining otter population- until her rescue in 1853. Despite this enduring myth, historians believe otherwise. If Scott O'Dell found the Lone Woman's story worthy enough to write a fictionalized tale, then what's to say her story was too enticing for journalists to pass up? After sifting through document after document, historians were surprised to discover the story of the Lone Woman was not only well known throughout California before 1853 but there were continual visitations to San Nicolas for years. The Lone Woman was famous, and she did not even know it! So how did her story reach the country?

On January 7, 1847, the *Boston Daily Atlas* released an article about the Lone Woman's story called *A Female Crusoe*. The word Crusoe comes from the fictional protagonist *Robinson Crusoe*. In the novel, *Robinson Crusoe* became stranded on a remote tropical island for years scavenging to survive while fighting off cannibals, mutineers, and captives! Crusoe, like Karana, was based on a real-life castaway named Alexander Selkirk; who lived alone on a tropical island for four years. *The Boston Daily Atlas* went to great lengths to re-tell the Lone Woman's story as a beautifully descriptive thriller for readers across the country.

> *"A Female Crusoe…. Some ten or twelve years after the departure of the Kodiaks, this tribe had become diminished to about twenty or thirty individuals, when the governor of the department of California sent over a*

*small vessel and removed them to the main[land]. In the
last boat, which was embarking with the last of the people,
(some six or eight perhaps in number), to convey them to
the vessel, which was to carry them from the home of their
nativity forever, was one of the tribe, small in stature, not
far advanced in years, and his dusky mate, then in the
bloom of life...She turned, to give the last lingering look
to her departing helpmate; and then, gathering around
her form her flowing mantle, wet by the ocean wave,
in an instant disappeared forever from the sight of her
astonished and sorrowing companions."*

Unfortunately for the Lone Woman, *royal furs* were still a hot
commodity on the international market. As soon as the island's
otter population sprung back to healthy numbers, hunters hastily
sailed to collect their prize.

Captured

It is difficult to ascertain the years the Lone Woman was spotted
by visitors- since the 1847 edition of the *Boston Daily Atlas*
records only a recap of the story- but these events must have
occurred within 12 years. Historians can only go off what writers
wrote at the time and try to fill in the missing gaps themselves.
Sometime between 1836 and 1847, the Lone Woman was going
about her daily routine when she saw another schooner on the
horizon heading straight towards the island. Could this be the
ship that would take them off the island? Unfortunately for the
Lone Woman, this ship and its crew were not there to rescue them
but instead came for otters.

  The Boston Daily Atlas records how many visitations to San
Nicolas Island. *"Since our, Crusoe became the sole monarch of the
isle, and Nicolas has been visited perhaps ten or twelve different times,
by different individuals; but there she has continued to be found, with
none to dispute her right — alone, solitary and forsaken."* However,
these new visitors were not always hunting parties. These

visitations ranged from regular fur hunters to illegal traders smuggling alcohol from the west indies- to avoid paying Mexican taxes. Seeing these visitors as their rescue party, the Lone Woman made herself known to them, yet these men were just as awful as the Russians.

Upon seeing an unlikely resident, the hunting party snatched the Lone Woman against her will and tied her up. From there, she was taken back with them to their camp as their new prize. This ordeal probably left the Lone Woman petrified at the prospects these men would take her off the island and leave her still small son alone unprotected. However, there was one good man who decided to let her go. Once released, the Lone Woman fled back to wherever home she made for her and her son and quickly relocated to the cave.

The cave became their permanent residence and provided perfect camouflage from their would-be capturers. After that day, the Lone Woman hid from visitors yet grew more difficult as the island continued to have frequent visitations.

Attempts To Get Her Off The Island

Within the twelve years, there would be more visitations to San Nicolas. These newcomers did encounter the Lone Woman and tried- through good intentions- to take her away from her loneliness on San Nicolas Island. However, the Lone Woman refused to go with them.

> "At the approach of the white man she flees, as from an evil spirit; and the only way to detain her is by running her down, as you would the wild goat of the mountain or the young fawn of the plains."

It stands to reason why the Lone Woman ran away from visitors: she was scared. After the ordeal she endured the first time, the Lone Woman grew scared of being captured again by those who would take her away from her son. These visitors further elaborated as to what she wore and her current location.

"Her dress, or covering, is composed of the skins of small birds, which she kills with stones, and sews them together with a needle of bone and the light sinews of the hair seal…. She never remains long in one spot; but is constantly wandering around the shores of the island, sleeping, which she seldom does, in small caves and crevices in the rocks."

It appears these visitors took an interest into the Lone Woman and tried to communicate with her. However, these communications ended before they even started.

"Every endeavor has been made, and every inducement offered, by different individuals, to prevail upon her to leave the island, but in vain. The only home she appears to desire, is her own little isle. Her last hope, if she has any, is, to finish her journey alone. She has no wish now, to hear again the sweet music of speech. Its sounds are no longer music to her ear and, as for civilized man, his tameness is shocking even to her dormant senses."

At first, she was afraid to talk with them and hid. She could not tell if these visitors had good or nefarious intentions. However, she still believed she had to face her fears and make herself known because she desperately wanted to be with her people again.

 When she finally made up her mind to make herself known it was always too late. By the time she made it to the shore, the ships were already gone. She found herself weeping even more for not making herself known. Each time, she self-sabotaged any attempt to get off San Nicolas Island.

The Death Of The Lone Woman's Son
In *Island of the Blue Dolphins*, Karana stumbles upon the lifeless body of her little brother Ramo- his throat ripped from a battle between the wild dogs. But this shocking moment in the story

was another inspiration from the Lone Woman's story. When Nidever inquired as to what happened to her son, the Lone Woman claimed the island's wild dogs took her baby and "torn" him to shreds.

> *"She related that when she went back after her child, she wandered a long time without finding it; that she concluded that the dogs had eaten the child, she lay down and cried for a long time and became sick, could not eat anything, and got so weak that she could not walk; that she recovered so she could get around, and began to eat."*

It was this interpretation that became the de facto explanation why Nidever or Dittman did not see the Lone Woman's child. However, in more recent years, a new story completely changes the narrative of what happened to the Lone Woman's son. According to Barbareño Chumash elder, Ernestine Ygnacio De-Soto, her great grandmother claimed to have met the Lone Woman and learned what had happened to her son.

The Adventures of Robinson Crusoe

For many seasons, the Lone Woman and her son lived on the island together. Then on a cloudless day, the Lone Woman's son was offshore fishing when something struck his canoe- either by a whale or shark- and vanished. Her son either drowned or was eaten by a shark. What's particularly interesting about the story of the death of the Lone Woman's child is the idea that she had not one son but two sons. One theory suggests that on moving day, the Lone Woman had two boys: a small boy and a baby.

On paper, the idea of the Lone Woman having two sons seems plausible. For starters, on moving day, when the Nicoleño reached the beach, the Lone Woman would have held her baby. From there, the Lone Woman notices her eldest son not with her and goes finding him- while carrying her baby- and later finds him hiding in the bushes. After the schooner departed the island, the Lone Woman was responsible for raising both her sons.

If the baby did perish from the wild dogs, then the Lone Woman still had another son to raise; and would have been content to stay on the island forever to raise her son. It would line up with De-Soto's claim that the Lone Woman's son had died sometime before her rescue. However, many experts are not convinced. First, they point out that those who encountered the Lone Woman- written 30 years after her death- could barely understand her signs. Also, the story could have changed within the 30 years-making the likelihood of the real story lost in translation.

Second, if the Lone Woman had two children, then how did the baby get taken away and eaten by the wild dogs? Did she turn her back and the dogs snatched the baby? Was she ambushed? Unfortunately, historians do not know. Lastly, if the story of the Lone Woman jumping off the *Peor es Nada* to find her baby is true, then she left her eldest son- presuming he did board the schooner-all alone with strangers. By the time the Lone Woman made her way back to the shore, she was now alone.If these theories are true, then the story of the Lone Woman must undergo another reevaluation; however, until new evidence comes to light, experts agree-for the time being- she had one son who died from accidental drowning.

We may never know the year the Lone Woman's son died or his age. This may explain why the *Boston Daily Atlas* does not mention any sighting of her son- or that he was still alive but hiding in a cave somewhere on the island.With the death of her son, any hopes the Lone Woman had of getting off the island together were squashed forever. Even the *Boston Daily Atlas* took note of her lonely existence.

> *"To all appearance, she is strong, healthy, and content to be alone. What can reconcile her to her lot, who can conjecture? Humanity may hope that contentment may continue to be hers, to the last hour; for she is destined to lie down and die alone, on the cold shore of her isolated home, with no one to administer to her last wants, and none to cover her cold body when the spirit shall have left the day..."*

Knowing her fate, the Lone Woman made peace that she would die alone. It seemed the Lone Woman was destined to fade into the annals of history, but history had other plans.

CHAPTER EIGHT

"If only I had not wondered about my sister Ulape, where she was, and if the marks she had drawn upon her cheeks had proved magical. If they had, she was now married to Nanko and was the mother of many children. She would have smiled to see all of mine, which were so different from the ones I always wished to have."

- ISLAND OF THE BLUE DOLPHINS (CHAPTER TWENTY-FIVE)

Whenever discussions about the Lone Woman's story arose amongst historians, one question continued popping up: why didn't Captain Hubbard return to San Nicolas to pick up the castaways? One week after dropping off the remaining Nicoleños in San Pedro, Hubbard began preparations to return to San Nicolas to pick up the Lone Woman and her child when he received an urgent order to come to Santa Barbara.

Hubbard was to take Captain Nidever and his hunting party to hunt otters on Santa Rosa Island. Which begs another question: why couldn't Captain Hubbard make a slight detour to pick up the Lone Woman and her son? Was he on a deadline? Or did he decide to forget her? Hubbard may have considered these questions himself, however, the *Peor es Nada* was in urgent demand along the Californian coast. If he chose to disobey orders and go back to San Nicolas, then the Lone Woman would've been alone only a couple weeks; instead of 18 years. Her story would have ended right there as an accident and simply forgotten in California history.

As soon as he completed his task, Hubbard intended to go to San Nicolas, however, he received another order to carry a cargo of timber from Monterey to the port of San Francisco. Captain Hubbard begrudgingly followed orders; hoping as soon as he dropped off the timber in San Francisco, he could go back to San Nicolas for the Lone Woman and her son. From his perspective, delaying their rescue for another week was a crime against justice and humanity.

Unfortunately for Captain Hubbard, he would never get the chance. When the *Peor es Nada* was nearing the entrance to the Golden Gate, the large schooner struck an object and capsized. Hubbard's men, exhausted from this ordeal, washed ashore, and watched as the remains of the *Peor es Nada* drifted out into the Pacific- where its pieces were salvaged by the Russians.

With the loss of the Monterey schooner, it was decided no schooner larger than fishing boats or canoes could go out onto the coast or to San Nicolas Island. *"...the only craft on the coast were small boats to which the long-distance and rough sea of the outer rim of the Channel would render a trip extremely dangerous."* Those eager to return to San Nicolas to rescue the castaways lost interest; believing both mother and child had died waiting for their return. No one was willing to risk traversing shark invested ocean to get to San Nicolas Island and rescue a Lone Woman and her child.

She Is Still Out There

Three years after the *Boston Daily Atlas* published their hit piece on the Lone Woman, sightings of her grew silent. Those who visited the island claimed to not finding any signs of her whereabouts and believed she may have died or eaten by the wild dogs. While others gave up the search for the Lone Woman, a group of tender-hearted padres of Mission Santa Barbara still believe she was alive on San Nicolas. The thought of her all alone on the island weighed heavily on their hearts. They felt guilty that one of God's children was left behind to suffer in the wilderness and believed it was their Christian duty to rescue the Lone Woman before it was too late.

However, not everyone was on board with the padres. Many

claim it been too long since they last saw her on the island. But in 1850, a returning hunting party relayed a story that San Nicolas was haunted by a ghost! One claimed they saw a wraith like figure of a woman standing on top of the cliffs coldly staring down at them; with another claiming to see the same ghost dashing across the moonlit beach. The next day, the hunting party found footprints along the beach shoreline.

> *"After the discovery of gold, it was rumored that San Nicolas was inhabited, and this, no doubt, had its foundation in the fact that several hunters of the sea otter, had seen the print of human footsteps, and they endeavored to discover the whereabouts of the individuals, but could not; yet as all the footprints were alike, they concluded that there could be only one person living upon it."*

These new sightings renewed Father Jose Maria de Jesus Gonzales' faith that the ghost the men had saw was the Lone Woman. This misunderstood sighting affirmed Gonzales' faith that she was still alive on the island.

Mission Santa Barbara

In 1852, Gonzales located an emissary named Thomas Jefferies- an English mariner who lived in Santa Barbara- to help search for the Female Crusoe. Jefferies had come into possession of a small schooner that could make it to San Nicolas Island. All the padres of Mission Santa Barbara paid Jefferies $200 to bring the woman or her child back to Santa Barbara alive. A new search for the Lost Woman of San Nicolas Island had begun.

George Nidever

Before they set sail to San Nicolas Island, Thomas Jefferies needed experts who had been on the island before. He enlisted fur hunter captain George Nidever and his crew as the captain for this expedition. Originally from Tennessee, George Nidever was an experienced adventurer, hunter, and fur trapper when he emigrated to California in 1834- traveling with the Walker Party, the first group to cross the Sierra Nevada and into California. Upon his arrival in Mexican California, Nidever began his pursuit of becoming a self-made man; through hunting for royal furs, starting up a sheep ranch, and raising stock.

However, due to stringent Mexican laws, foreigners like Nidever could not claim any land for themselves unless they were Mexican citizens and Catholic. Wanting to live in California badly, Nidever decided to become a Mexican citizen. First, Nidever received his Catholic baptism on January 27, 1842. The following year on February 13, 1841, he married a native Californio named María Sinforosa Ramona Sanchez- whose family owned a 14, 000-acre Rancho called Santa Clara Rio del Norte A frontiersman and mountain man, Nidever spent most of his time in the natural world and became an expert at hunting animals of the Pacific West.

Fur Hunter George Nidever

While living in California, Nidever had heard the story of the Lone Woman- that captured his imagination- and wanted to bet the one to find her.In 1843, Nidever, alongside Thomas Sparks- who returned eight years after the Nicoleno's departure- traveled to San Nicolas to hunt for otter and help Sparks locate the Lone Woman, but without a map of the island, looking for the Lone Woman was like looking for a needle in a haystack. They did not find her except for her footprints on the beach.Even though they found tangible evidence she was close by, Nidever and Sparks decided not to follow through with their investigation and returned to hunting otter. However, when Jefferies asked for his assistance, Nidever was determined to find her.

First Visit
Captain Nidever, his crew, and Jefferies set sailed for San Nicolas Island in the spring of 1852 to locate the Lone Woman. *"In April of 1852, I went over to the Islands with my schooner, accompanied by a foreigner by name of Tom Jeffries, who is still living here, and 2 Indians, for sea gull's eggs. These eggs were in great demand at that time.* While his party was searching for sea gull eggs, Nidever did some exploring- hoping to find the Lone Woman close to their vicinity- and across the remains of *Tule Creek.* As he examined the abandon site, Nidever noticed three windbreaks that had several poles- ranging from 7-8ft- with pieces of seal blubber stuck on top

of them.

> "At a distance of a few hundred yards, back from the
> beach and about 2 miles apart, we found 3 small circular
> enclosures, made of sage brush.... Outside the huts,
> however, we found signs of the place having been visited
> not many months before. Around each hut and a short
> distance from where it was several stakes or poles, usually
> from 4 to 6, some 7 or 8 feet high, which were standing
> upright in the ground, and pieces of seal blubber stuck on
> the top of each."

In Nidever's eyes this could mean only one thing: the Lone
Woman was in the vicinity and was drying out blubber for later
use. Nidever theorized the Lone Woman was working on drying
seal blubber before their schooner had landed. After a few hours
of looking, Nidever failed to locate the Lone Woman albeit her
footprints.

> "We went direct to the San Nicolas, and having arrived
> early in the day, Jeffries, one of the Indians, and I landed
> and traveled along the beach towards the upper end of
> the island some 6 or 7 miles. At a short distance from the
> beach, about 200 yards, we discovered the footprints of
> a human being, probably of a woman as they were quite
> small. They had evidently been made during the previous
> rainy season as they were well defined and sunk quite deep
> into the soil then soft, but now dry and hard."

Despite finding her footprints, Nidever wanted to keep looking
for, but had to leave the island when a convenient storm picked
up. For the next 8 days, Nidever had to wait on board to return to
San Nicolas.

After the storm passed, Nidever returned to collect sea gull
eggs, but due to the storm, could not find any gull eggs. With the
weather getting worse, Nidever had no choice but to leave San

Nicolas and return to the mainland empty handed, but as they were leaving, Nidever swore he saw a pale ghostly figure dancing in the frothy seafoam.

Second Visit

Although Nidever failed to locate the Lone Woman, the fact he found evidence of activity on San Nicolas reaffirmed the padres' faith that she did not perish. *"Upon my return from my first trip, I told several persons that we had seen several footprints on the island, and Father Gonzalez of the Mission, having heard of it, requested me to make all possible search for her."* In the winter of 1852, Nidever led his crew back to San Nicolas for their second attempt to find the Lone Woman. *"We landed near the lower end of the island and, as I and Jefferies had done, we proceeded along the beach towards the head of the island, leaving our Indians in charge of the boat."*

On his second visit, Nidever was accompanied by his good Charles Dittman- who will play an essential role in the discovery of the Lone Woman- and hoped this time they would find her. *"We had decided to go the head of the island, as, for various reasons, we concluded that if alive she would be mostly likely to be found there."* Nidever theorized since the water at the head of the island was more abundant, the likely chance the Lone Woman was there hunting for fish and seal.

As he passed by *Tule Creek,* Nidever noticed the seal blubber- that were on the poles on his previous visit- had disappeared and was replaced by fresh blubber. The Lone Woman was around the area. Nidever and Dittman decided to venture forward.Within half a mile of the head of the island, Nidever and Dittman came across a low sandy flat- that extended from one side of the island to the next. Both hunters believe the Lone Woman had to have lived in this area. After searching for a while, Nidever and Dittman did not find any sightings of the *Wild Woman*; however, Dittman came across something in the brush.

"After searching around for some time and finding no

signs of her, we were about to return, having concluded that the dogs must have eaten her, as not even her bones were to be found, when I discovered in the crotch of a bush or small tree a basket, and upon throwing off the piece of seal skin that covered it, we found within carefully laid together, a dress made of shag skins cut in square pieces, a rope made of sinew, and several smaller articles, such as abalone fish hooks, bone needles etc."

While they did not find the Lone Woman per say, Dittman got an idea. "After examining them, Brown proposed replacing them and returning the basket to the tree where we found it, but I scattered them about on the ground, telling him that if upon our return we should find them replaced in the basket, it would be proof of the woman's existence."

After completing his task, Dittman and Nidever headed back to camp, but as they made their way through the beach, they stumbled upon fresh barefooted footprints. It appeared the Lone Woman was nearby watching them like a hawk. For the next two daya, Nidever's hunting party hunted for otter- all the while looking for signs of their ghostly friend- and did not find any signs of her. With the weather taking a turn for the worse, Nidever had no choice but to leave San Nicolas for the island of San Miguel. Once the gale ceased its rage, Nidever returned to Santa Barbara; another failure on his Lone Woman rescue plan. Doubts crept into his mind that it was a waste of time and money to look for a phantom.

However, padre Gonzalez was not giving up. He still had faith the Lone Woman was still alive on the island. If Nidever could not find her, then Gonzales would get someone else; and if that person failed, he would find someone else until she is brought safely to Santa Barbara. "Upon my return from my first trip I told several persons that we had seen several footprints on the island, and Father Gonzales of the Mission, having heard of it, requested me to make all possible search for her."

Nidever decided to take a break and return home to his ranch until the summer of 1853; when Father Gonzales urged him to go to San Nicolas one more time to find the Lone Woman. Even though he wanted to say no to the padres, Nidever still believed she was still alive and agreed to look for her for one last season. Nidever's crew consisted of Carl Dittman, an Irish cook named Colorado, four mission Indians- named Policarpio, Melquiades, Hilario, and an unknown Indian. It would be Dittman- and not Nidever- who discovered the Lone Woman.

Carl Dittman

A majority of what is about to happen comes from Carl Dittman's *Narrative of a Seafaring Life on The Coast of California (1878.)* Who was Carl Dittman? Carl August Dittman was born in Berlin, Prussia on the 7th of November 1825. As a citizen of Prussia, Dittman was expected to serve in the military, however, he felt the open sea calling out to him. He decided to become a sailor. In 1844, Dittman slipped out of Prussia under the guise of Carl 'Charley' Brown and emigrated to Monterey, California- in the fall of 1845. However, in 1846, Dittman was arrested- under laws set by the Mexican government on foreigners- in Santa Barbara but later was released because he was not an American.

For several years, Dittman sailed the Pacific hunting otters alongside veteran otter hunter George Nidever. The two became close friends. By 1853, Dittman had become an expert sailor and otter hunter and would go with Nidever to find the Lone Woman, but little did both men know, he would be the one to find her.

The Final Visit

After making anchorage on the eastern side of San Nicolas in August of 1853, Nidever and his crew made their way to the sandspit.

> *"...We went first to San Miguel, & thence to San Nicolas, where we arrived early in the afternoon. We came to anchor on the N.E. side about the middle of the Island. As*

soon as we came to anchor Nidever & I went on shore for the purpose of seeing where the otter lay & also to pick out a site for our camp as we intended to make a long stay & would move onshore the next day." As they walked, the hunting party encountered the skeletal remains of Tule Creek. *"From this point, we saw further up the ridge three huts. Upon reaching them we found them made of whale bones, covered with brush, although they were now open on all sides."*

Nidever decided to set up a camp- where they hoped to stay for at least 2-3 months- not too far from *Tule Creek* called *Ranch House Landing*. He theorized the Lone Woman could be close to her old village and wanted to be as close as possible to catch her. As the crew was setting up camp, Dittman explored the abandoned huts and came across a basket full of feathers and got an idea.

 While the party began setting into *Ranch House Landing*, Nidever and Ditman decided to explore the island coast for signs of the Lone Woman. As they explored, both men came across wild dogs. *"On the way, we saw several dogs that looked much like a coyote excepting in color which was black & white; they were quite wild & ran away as soon as we came into sight."* A couple of hours went by, and there were no signs of the Lone Woman's whereabouts. Needing to rest, Nidever and Dittman stopped at a spring- referred to today as *Old Gardens*- to get some fresh water.

 While Nidever decided to stay behind and rest, Dittman continued exploring until he reached the western end of the island. After spending a couple hours exploring, Dittman failed to find any presence of the Lone Woman's and decided to head back. As he was walking back to *Old Gardens*, Dittman stumbled upon some familiar-looking footprints. *"Not far from the head I found footprints leading from the beach up over the bank & thence up to the ridge above. I followed them until they disappeared in a kind of moss with which the ground was covered, a short distance above the bank."*Curious seeing footprints seeing this high up, Dittman continued up a little further- from the beach up over the ridge- until he came to one side of the ridge where he lost them.

However, he discovered a piece of driftwood. Perplexed how a piece of driftwood got this far up inland from the beach, Dittman concluded it was not one the mission Indians, but had to have been the Lone Woman; meaning she was close by. When Dittman relayed his discovery to Nidever, he was convinced the Lone Woman had to be close by.

> *"As it was growing late, I returned to where I had left Nidever & reported what I had seen. He said at first that they might be the tracks of our Indians, but he afterwards admitted that it was impossible for them to have got ahead of us, & I too was sure that the footprints were too small for those of a man."*

Although ecstatic at the prospects of the Lone Woman being alive from Dittman's report, Nidever already made up his mind. After being let down so many times, he believed they were too late, and she probably been eaten by the wild dogs they have encountered on their walk. *"Nidever, however, was not very sanguine about finding her. He had concluded that the dogs had eaten her & was very doubtful if even her bones could be found."*

That evening, as Nidever and Dittman strolled the beaches enjoying their pipes, they spotted something on the beach. There, on that warm limpid night- when the stars are at their brightest- the blaze of the moon's moonlight outlined on the lonely shore slender footprints. It was the Lone Woman! Nidever was stunned.

"The Woman of San Nicolas! My God, she is living!"

Then, Nidever remembered when he left the island on his first voyage, he saw a ghostly figure on the beach shore; and then it hit him: what he saw wasn't a ghostly apparition, but the Lone

Woman herself!

He concluded that she was nearby their camp the day they left. The footprints were more than enough evidence to convince Nidever the Lone Woman was still roaming the island. With his hopes restored, Nidever informed the crew to get some good rest; for they are going to catch the Lone Woman once and for all.

CHAPTER NINE

"I live contented, because I see the day when I want to get out of this island."

-   THE LONE WOMAN OF SAN NICOLAS ISLAND

It was a clear morning when Nidever, Dittman, Policarpio, Melquiades, Colorado, and Hilario ate their breakfast. Their spirits were high for today they would find their elusive ghost. As soon as they finished consuming their meal, the men headed to *Old Gardens*. There was no cloud in the sky but a gentle breeze dancing off their garbs. After discovering the ghost like footprints, the night before, Nidever was convinced the Lone Woman was somewhere on the opposite end of the island- where access was difficult.

Once settled, Nidever orders Dittman to take the three Indians to the spot where he found the basket and the footprints and see if there were any new traces of the Lone Woman; while he and Colorado would proceed down the island and scope the beaches of her presence. A few hours went by on the quiet beach with no signs of the Lone Woman. As Nidever combed the beaches for the Lone Woman, Dittman returned to the other side of the island- believing she had to be close by-was dismayed to not finding any signs.

He then ordered the Indians to look around the area while he Dittman went ahead to check if the footprints were still there. *"I did not return with them, but I went up that side of the Island until I struck the footprints, I had discovered the day before."* By the time he got to the spot- after a dangerous climb over some slippery rocks- Dittman could see the footprints- but no driftwood. Dittman, now with more time to explore, decided to follow the footprints and see where they would take him.

"I followed the tracks up over the bank & from the point where they could no longer be seen continued to ascend the ridge. About halfway up I found a small piece of driftwood which I concluded she must have dropped on her way from the beach with fire wood."

After locating the missing driftwood, Dittman unknowingly stumbled upon three mysterious whale bone windbreaks.

"From where I found the piece of driftwood, I could see three huts further up the ridge & having gone up to them I found them constructed of whales' ribs & covered with brush although they were open all around & the high grass growing within them showed that they could not have been occupied for some time."

What surprised Dittman about the location of the three windbreaks was its position. The three windbreaks were located at the western end of the island- called the *'Great Sand Dunes'*- and was a perfect spot for the Lone Woman.

For starters, the *San Dunes* had a panoramic view of the Pacific Ocean where the Lone Woman could see incoming schooners, was a viable spot to hunt sea lions, western gulls, and cormorants. Nearby was the *Old Garden* spring which made the area suitable for two to three people.

Dittman even saw the others wandering around looking for the Lone Woman. *"From this point, I could look over the whole length & breadth of the ridge & sand flat beyond where I could plainly see our men moving around."* As he got closer to the windbreaks, Dittman noticed some movement. At first, he thought it was the wild dogs scavenging for leftover food- presumably left by the Lone Woman- but on closer inspection, the crow like figure moved like a person. It was the Lone Woman!

> *"I began to look about me & finally discovered at a distance on the N.E. side of the ridge & about halfway to its top, a small black object that from where I stood looked like a crow seated on a bush. I thought I saw it move, & so went towards it. I soon discovered that it was the Indian woman."*

While that was going on, Policarpio, Hilario, and Melquiades were looking for the Lone Woman, they happened to stumble upon the seal skin basket Ditmman discovered the previous year. However, the contents Dittman purposely scattered- originally to lure out the Lone Woman- had vanished. They removed the leathery seal skin to find all the contents back in the basket. Dittman was right: the Lone Woman was nearby.

As the men checked the basket, one of them claimed to have seen a dark phantom struggling to get up a hill. The figure appeared to be carrying something heavy and was heading near the direction where Dittman had seen the footprints and driftwood. By the time they followed the massive shadow, Dittman was able to see them. With the Lone Woman in his periphery, Dittman returned to the Old Garden to inform Nidever of her location. It was time to meet the Lone Woman face to face.

Meeting The Lone Woman

Dittman, not waiting for his men or Nidever, decided to get a little closer to see the Lone Woman. *"She was seated within an enclosure similar to those already described so that until quite near her I could only see her head & shoulders. I approached her cautiously & was enabled to get within a few yards of her unobserved as she had her face turned from the direction in which I had come."* Dittman further elaborates the Lone Woman was not alone as originally thought.

"I approached her cautiously & was enabled to get within a few yards of her unobserved as she had her face turned from the direction in which I had come. While I was still some distance away two dogs, probably the same we had seen the day before began to growl whereupon she gave a yell & they went away; but she did not turn around."

It appeared that the Lone Woman- either before or after the death of her son- had domesticated two dogs to act as her companions and guards. What's interesting about these dogs was the fact she had two.

Normally one dog would be good enough to act as a companion, fend off visitors or other wild dogs, but what purpose did the second dog have? Could the second dog be the young pup of the other dog? Or did both dogs symbolize the Lone Woman's two- though still a theory- dead children? Unfortunately, we will never know the true importance of these two dogs were to the Lone Woman, yet it's likely they were her companions. Although he was on his own, Dittman could see Nidever and the crew scattering around the sand flats like ants and signaled them to his location.

"From this point I could plainly see our men searching about on the sandy flat, & I signaled to them by placing my hat on the ramrod of my gun & raising & lowering it until I succeeded in attracting their attention, when I made signs for them to come."

While Nidever and co. was getting into position, Dittman had enough time to observe what the Lone Woman was working on.

"She was seated cross legged on the ground & was engaged in separating the blubber from a piece of seal skin which was lying across one knee & held by one hand. In the other hand she grasped a crude knife, a piece of iron hoop thrust

into a rough piece of wood for a handle & held so that the back of the hand was turned down, scraping & cutting from, instead of towards her. Just outside the enclosure there was a high pile of ashes & bones showing that she had lived in this place some time."

Dittman- and later Nidever- noted her elegant cormorant dress.

"Her covering consisted of a single garment of the shag's [cormorant] skin, the feathers out & pointing downward, in shape resembling a loose gown. It was sleeveless, low in the neck & was girded at the waist with sinew rope. When she stood up, as I afterwards observed, it extended nearly to her ankles. She had no covering on her head; her hair which was thickly matted, & bleached & a reddish brown, hung down to her shoulders."

Despite watching her work her magic, Dittman was concerned once she laid eyes on him, or the crew would run away. *"The old woman saw them also, as every few minutes she would look toward the flat, shading her eyes from the sun with her hand & talking rapidly to herself."*Dittman signaled to the party to make a circle formation- this allowed the men to catch the Lone Woman on all sides if she chose to run.

After everyone was in position, Dittman moved in. As he began moving in, Dittman feared the Lone Woman-having seen Nidever and his men moving across the flat-would take one look at him and attempt to run away. Years prior, the *Boston Daily Atlas* reported the Lone Woman was fearful of visitors and refused to be formal with them, but in a remarkable twist, the Lone Woman- seeing Dittman approaching her- was excited to see him.

"While they were still some distance away, but sufficiently near to prevent her escape, I stepped around in front of her, but instead of seeing her startled & alarmed, I was surprised to have her bow & smile, as though it was a

delight to see me & my visit an everyday occurrence. She began a rapid talking & gesticulating, all of which was wholly unintelligible to me."

When she saw the rest of the hunting party approach, the Lone Woman got even more excited.

"As fast as the men approached her, she also bowed, smiled & talked to them." But what made her heart sing the most was seeing other Indians for the first time in nearly two decades. She then welcomed the crew into her home and made food for the entire party."

Dittman then notes how the Lone Woman wanted the hunting party to eat.

"They all sat down in a circle around her while I made signals to Nidever who was in sight to come to us. After some delay he came up & we sat down with the men. Taking some roots from two bags or sacks made of grass she placed them in the coals & as soon as they were roasted, she passed them around making motions for us to eat. One of the roots was what is commonly called carcomite among the Californians; the other I do not know the name of."

Dittman and Nidever asked the Indians to try and communicate with her using their language, yet the Lone Woman could not understand their language. *"The Indians among our men tried to talk with the old woman but did not succeed in making themselves understood, neither could they comprehend her language."* Despite the lack of communication, the Lone Woman was happy to see Indians again.

Relocating The Lone Woman

After being formal with her, Captain Nidever wanted to get the Lone Woman to come back with them. He asked the Indians if they should use force to take her, but they disagreed with this idea. *"Nidever asked the Indians if they thought the old woman could be taken by force if necessary. They replied that there would be no difficulty."* While Nidever believed force was the best option, Dittman thought persuasion was the better alternative.

> *"Hearing this I told Nidever I did not think that there would be any necessity of using force, & that if she could be made to understand what was wanted that she would willingly go with us. Patting her on the shoulder to attract her attention I went through the motions of packing her things in to the baskets, placing this on my back & walking off in the direction of the beach, & then said vamos the Spanish for let us go."*

Dittman further elaborates:

> *"The motions she no doubt understood, but the word vamos seemed to be more intelligible, as upon hearing it her face brightened up & she set to work with alacrity to get ready. She filled her baskets & in the larger one she placed the seal's head after replacing the putrid brains & tearing away from its bits of adhering flesh. This basket she raised to her back & secured with straps passing over her shoulders & under her arms. She took other articles in her hands & started off towards the beach with a load that seemed heavy enough for a mule."*

However, fears began crawling like millipedes at the back of Nidever and Dittman's skulls. They feared she was being too nice so when their backs were turned, she would dash off. *"Two of our Indians went ahead of her while Nidever & I brought up the rear to guard against any attempt escape, although no such precaution was necessary."* After gathering her belongings, the group set out to Ranch House Landing. Along the way, the Lone Woman gave the small party a special tour to sites she regularly stops at.

> *"Upon reaching the beach we stopped at a spring that*

*forms a little pool of water under a sort of mound of
rocks & situated but a few yards from the beach. One
of the peculiarities of this spring was its surface, which
is at all times ruffled with a cool breeze which seems to
be continually playing over the pool. I noticed it on this
occasion & at several times afterwards. The water was
invariably clear & cool. Its source I should judge must have
been high up on the ridge."*

First, she led the party to the Old Garden to get something to
drink. Dittman notes the Lone Woman showing the crew what
she had left behind in the rocks near the spring.

*"Around this spring were several poles erected & on these
we hung the things we had brought from the old woman's
place, for each of us had our hands full, & made motions
for the old woman to do the same. We hung the things up
very carefully & the old woman followed our example,
without, to all appearances, the least reluctance. In the
cracks & fissures of the rocks that formed the mound we
found thrust numbers of bones which we afterwards came
to the conclusion had been placed there by the old woman,
to furnish her food in time of need."*

Ditmman continues:

*"I afterwards noticed that she always saved the bones
contained in her food, placing them in baskets, to be taken
out at intervals & sucked until they were cleaned of every
particle of meat. She also saved the scraps of food that
were left & ate them when she felt hungry. She ate very
little at a time, but took food several times during the day."*

It appeared the Lone Woman made a contingency plan if she
ran out of food, was too sick or injured to hunt, to preserve the
bones of larger animals she killed because its marrow acted as a

secondary food source. However, she had to place the extra food in a higher elevation. The island was teeming with wild dogs, and they were pronged to eat whatever they found, but placing the food higher up, made it impossible for the dogs to steal her food.

After leaving the *Old Garden*, the Lone Woman took them to another spring, called *Thousand Springs*, where she could bathe and clean herself up. *"From this spring we proceeded along the beach or rather on top of the bank until we arrived at a path that led down to another spring on the beach. The men who were still ahead continued along the bank, but the old woman went down the path to the spring. We saw she intended to wash herself, & so withdrew & waited until she returned when we continued along the bank to the boat."* While bathing, Nidever, and Ditman were still concerned she would escape again.

To squash their doubts, both men agreed when they get back to Ranch House Landing, they would immediately take her to their ship. With everyone on board, if the Lone Woman decided to change her mind, the men would stop her before she had the chance to jump off. But once again, the Lone Woman did not attempt to escape. Quite the opposite, she was more fascinated by what was on the ship.

> *"We made motions for her to get into the boat, which she did without any hesitation, & crawled forward to the bow, & there knelt down, holding on to the side with her hands. Arrived on board, she crept up to the galley or stove which was on deck & made signs that it was warm there."*

It looked like the Lone Woman was not going to leave any time soon. That night, Captain Nidever decided they should have dinner on the ship. *"We had dinner as soon as we got on board & gave the old woman some of our food."* She ate heartily & with an apparent relish & our food at this & in fact at all times seemed to agree with her."

Although Ditman, Nidever, and co. found her, they decided to camp on San Nicolas Island for two months hunting and learn everything about her day-to-day life and hunt otter. Dittman made the Lone Woman a dull petticoat so she could better blend with the rest of the crew. By putting her in a traditional dress, the Lone Woman could get accustomed to the feel of her new home-and to look more "civilize" in the eyes of Californians. The Lone Woman, having lived her entire life sleeveless, may have felt the lifeless dress too hot and constraining.

> *"That afternoon i buised myself on making a petticoat or skirt for her, out of ticking, & this with a man's skirt, a black necktie & an old cape or cloak that Nidever gave her completed the dress she afterwards wore while with us on the island."*

While Dittman was sewing, the Lone Woman could not help but laugh at the way he was using a needle and thread. Sitting next to him, she took out one of her bone needles and showed him how to puncture the fabric, but when she tried using the threaded needle, she could not thread the cloth correctly. This tender moment between Dittman and the Lone Woman demonstrates that although they come from two vastly different cultures, they found comfort in each other's company.

Getting To Know The Lone Woman

The next day, the crew made a makeshift hut for the Lone Woman. *"The following day we went on shore & put up a tent or shelter near the beach at a point already selected. Nearby we made a species of hut for the old woman, who seemed perfectly contented with us making no attempt to leave us, although the opportunity was not wanting."* During the two month's stay, the Lone Woman showed Nidever and Dittman the cave she used as a secondary home-and where she hid from hunters and visitors looking for her.

Through symbols, the Lone Woman tells the men how she lived

off fish, seal- and seals blubber- abalone, roots, cormorants, and corms. She also describes how she went back and forth from her windbreak home to her cave; drying meat at each station and storing the extra food into the crevices in case of emergencies. The Lone Woman later admits she hated hiding and not making herself more known to others- in fear of being taken against her will- and that was indeed her Nidever saw that stormy 1851 day.

The hunting party meeting the Lone Woman

For Captain Nidever, this was a revelation. The Lone Woman then revealed a stunning piece of information to Dittman and Nidever: the moment Dittman approached her, she was completely caught off guard and was going to flee, but due to their sudden arrival, she was trapped. Petrified, she composed herself and decided to not run away from her fear and comfort them- believing these men could take her to her people- and when she saw other Indians like herself, she went from being overtly anxious to feeling calm.

She knew she made the right choice. Nidever and Dittman probably let out a sigh of relief knowing their Indian compatriots made the difference! But why did the Lone Woman decide to leave now? Surely, she could have made herself known to Nidever the two times he visited the island looking for her? The most likely reason she chose to leave the island now was her son. She decided to stay behind on San Nicolas to be with and raise her son- to the best of her ability- in the ways of the Nicoleño, but when he died, there was no longer a reason to stay on the island. With her son dead, she could now go to San Pedro and be with her people or so she thought.

While Dittman and Nidever went hunting, the Lone Woman stayed at the campsite making baskets.

> *"The old woman remained in camp with the cook, one of the Mission Indians, the rest of us being away after otter the greater part of each day. The old woman's chief occupation was working on her baskets, of which she had several not yet completed, wandering about on the Island, or bringing wood & water."*

Captain Nidever and Dittman were astonished not only of the Lone Woman's incredible tenacity to live by herself for 18 tumultuous years but not go insane from loneliness.

She may not have said it, but the Lone Woman may have credited her survival to the teachings of her people- to whom she missed every day while on the island- her hopes to see them again, and her son. As the month trailed by, Nidever, Dittman, and the crew grew fondly of the Lone Woman and noted how caring she could be.

> *"She was always anxious to help when she saw an opportunity of making herself useful. She was always cheerful, & always talking & laughing. She took readily to our food & only on one occasion showed any disposition to return to her former food."*

For the first time in 18 years, the Lone Woman felt genuine happiness being around others once again, to laugh, to smile, to converse, to be human.

CHAPTER TEN

*"Then I did something that made me smile at myself. I did what
my older sister Ulape had done when she left the Island of the Blue
Dolphins. Below the mark of our tribe, I carefully made the sign which
meant that I was still unmarried. I was no longer a girl, yet I made it
anyway, using the blue clay and some white clay for the dots."*

- ISLAND OF THE BLUE DOLPHINS (CHAPTER 29)

In late August 1853, the schooner-lifting its hulking anchor
from the deep depths of the Pacific- departed San Nicolas Island
for the final time. As she looked back to her island one last
time-remembering all the good and the bad- the Lone Woman
was content to finally be off the island and going to the place
where her people were waiting to welcome her home; however,
California yet again changed hands. While the Lone Woman
scavenged for her next meal, California was seeing an increase in
American immigrants illegally settling in Mexican territory.

By 1845, thousands of Americans had settled in California,
and they were not happy with Mexico's restrictive laws- must
be Catholic or a Mexican citizen- in owning land. As a result,
many feared they would be evicted from their homes. Even the
governor, Pio Pico, despised the influx of Americans and warned
every Californio armed and prepared for an American invasion.
Little did Pico know his warning was going to come true.

Around the mid-1800s, the phrase *Manifest Destiny* took
America by storm. Coined after a magazine editor, *Manifest
Destiny* was the belief that it was America's destiny- and
entitlement- to claim the entirety of the North American

continent. Then in December 1845, U.S. General John C. Fremont, accompanied by 60 soldiers, arrived in California- under the guise of securing a suitable passageway through the Sierra mountains.

After being thrown out by Mexican commander, Jose Castro- who believed Fremont was spying- in March 1846, many Americans living in California took this as a sign they too would be evicted. Turns out Castro's assumption about Fremont was correct, he was spying and encouraging Americans to revolt. By April 1846, the United States had begun their three-year campaign against Mexico when California was dragged into the conflict.

From Mexican Hands To American Hands
On June 14, 1846, 90 armed American settlers led a successful revolt in Sonoma and easily captured the mayor and locked him up at *Sutter's Fort*. Once locked up, the American rebels hoisted a new flag with a grizzly bear declaring California as the *Bear Flag Republic of Independent California*. Now free from Mexico, Fremont- who had helped the rebels early on before the *Mexican-American War* broke out-returned to California and dissolved the new republic; placed the territory under the control of the U.S. government.

Many Californios welcomed the U.S. takeover, while others resented being controlled by Americans; however, the Indians were all to ecstatic- though they tried to remain neutral for as long as they could, but eventually were dragged into the conflict. Remembering their treatment under the Spanish and Mexicans, the Indians took their revenge by joining the Americans, raiding ranchos, and murdering Californio men, women, and children.
Then, on January 13th, 1847, Mexican Captain Jose Maria Flores surrendered California to Fremont. After the war officially ended in 1848, California would be stuck in limbo, yet its destiny changed when on January 24, 1848, gold was discovered near Sutter's Mill. In two years, California would undergo a major shift as 85,000 people from the continent and over the world made the

long trek to strike rich. Many succeeded, others failed.

Due to the influx of so many people, major cities like San Francisco, and Los Angeles ballooned in size. Unfortunately, the *Gold Rush* would be responsible for the massacre of Indians-those who lived deep in the woods and not forcibly taken into the missions or ranchos- as the new governor made the hunting and scalping not only legal, and profitable but acceptable amongst the populace. From their perspective, they were getting rid of the "pest" and reshaping California the way they wanted the state to look and feel- and for its citizens to live safely.Many Indians lives changed overnight. After the signing of *Treaty of Guadalupe Hidalgo* (1850), many Californians pressed for statehood of the territory.

On September 9, 1850, California become the 31st state of the United States as a free state- ending California's long history of slavery. As for the Californios, their lives were about to change for the worse. Like what happened to the missions under the Mexicans, the now American controlled California forced their changes onto the Californios. Rancheros were stripped of their political and financial powers, had to prove in court the lands they owned were legitimate, and had to pay large taxes. Eventually, the rancheros lost everything, while many Californian Indians faced an uncertain yet unequal future- the ramifications and consequences are still prevalent today.

Arriving In Santa Barbara
On the trip back to Santa Barbara, a gale overtook the Pacific. With no relief from the harsh winds, Captain Nidever decided to stop at Santa Cruz Island to wait out the storm.

> *"About a month later having secured something over 80 otter skins, & the otter having scattered we started on our return. We had barely left the Island when a gale sprang up so violent that several times we thought we should have to return to the Island. Late in the afternoon however we arrived in safety under the lee of Santa Cruz Island & the*

next morning early reached Santa Barbara."

While the storm raged its war on the Pacific, the Lone Woman made signs- to the crew- she would stop the winds through prayer and song. Everyone looked at her in disbelief. How could she stop a rampaging storm by singing for it to go away?

But the Lone Woman ignored their lack of faith and made her way to the center of the deck, got down on her knees, faced the wailing gale, and began singing and praying. Some laughed at this nonsense, but Nidever and Dittman were intrigued. After several exhaustive hours of praying and singing at the storm, the winds abruptly stopped; as the sun broke through the greyish clouds as its rays shined down on the ocean's reflective surface.

> *"When the gale sprang up after leaving the Island the old woman made signs to us that she was going to stop the wind. Accordingly she got down on her knees & remained so for some time apparently engaged in prayer, & facing in the direction of the wind. This she repeated several time during the day until the storm abated late in the afternoon, when turning to us she made signs that her prayers had been answered."*

The men- who laughed at this nonsense- on deck were stunned, while Nidever and Dittman were astounded. As they picked up their collective jaws off the deck, they scratched their heads how a lone Indian could calm a raging storm. In their eyes, it was as if the Lone Woman was praying to Saint Nicholas himself to protect them. They now saw the Lone Woman in a different light that day.

With the storm's rage abated, the exhausted party continued their journey to Santa Barbara and safely arrived on October 1, 1853. As they were approaching Santa Barbara harbor, the Lone Woman was caught off guard by more people riding horses, carts pulled by gigantic oxen, and many white people. *"On approaching the beach at Santa Barbara, she saw, evidently for the first time, an ox cart & a man on horseback."*

Seeing these strange animals caused a sense of wonder to swell within the Female Crusoe. *"At first sight of them, her delight was unbounded. She laughed and danced and continued to point at them & talk about them as long as they were in sight."* For most of her life, the Lone Woman only knew the plant and marine life of San Nicolas Island, yet seeing these new animals was all too exciting to her.

As the schooner made anchorage in Santa Barbara's harbor, Nidever's son- who had been on the lookout for his father's sails- rode down on a bronco to meet them. If seeing new animals and Nidever's son surprised the Lone Woman, then meeting the townspeople was an entirely different beast. When the citizens of Santa Barbara caught word of her arrival, they stormed the harbor to see the elusive Female Crusoe they periodically read in the papers.

> *"The story soon spread that the lost woman of the San Nicolas was found. The possibility of there being a woman living alone on a desert island, in the ocean, with only wild animals for companions, had been discussed in many households, and with such warm-hearted people was a subject of intense interest."*

Journalists who were at the harbor that day wrote a full description of the Lone Woman:

> *"She has a large, full eye; her forehead is low and broad; her nose slightly aquiline and finely formed; her mouth is rather large and indicates great firmness; her protruding lower lip gives a haughty tone to her look, and her well set chin fully sustains this trait. She is of medium stature, very masculine in appearance, and shows very little evidence of advanced age. Undoubtedly, she is the last of her race."*

Seeing all these people wanting to meet her may have made the Lone Woman feel more welcomed to her new homeland, yet she did not see any Nicoleño amongst the crowd. She hoped that the news of her arrival would make it to her people, and they would come to see her in her new home: the Nidever homestead.

Living With The Nidever
Having grown to care for her during their month stay on the island, Nidever decided to take the Lone Woman into his Rancho Santa Clara Rio del Norte. News of her arrival quickly spread from the harbor to Father Gonzales at Mission Santa Barbara.

> *"Hundreds flocked to Nidever's house. Among others came Fathers Gonzalez, Sanchez, and Jimeno ...One of the reverend clergymen of the Mission of Santa Barbara, accompanied by the writer, went to see her as soon as he heard of her arrival. He brought with him one of the Mission Indians who could speak the languages of one or two tribes of the California Indians. She was greatly delighted to see this Indian, but neither of them could understand a word of what the other said...."*

Despite the language barrier, Father Gonzales was delighted to see the Lone Woman alive, safe, and jubilant. Even the neighboring rancheros galloped their way to the Santa Clara Rio del Norte to meet the Lone Woman in person.Meeting even more people may have made the Lone Woman feel happy-just to be around others again- to laugh, smile, and be part of a family. She even shared some of her culture.

> *"She is very contented and takes great delight in showing to her visitors as well as she can, how she dug the roots, caught the fish, manufactured her garments, and provided generally for her sustenance. She signifies that she is much better pleased with her present mode of life than she led on*

the island."

However, she hadn't forgotten her reason for coming here. She made signs to Nidever about wanting to see her people, but Nidever did not know the location of the Nicoleño in Santa Barbara.

Dismayed, the Lone Woman gladly waited for Nidever to bring her any news about the whereabouts of her people. While she waited, a brig called the *Fremont* made port in Santa Barbara. The captain, hearing news of the Lone Woman's arrival- and knowing her story-offered Nidever $1000 to take her off his hands and put her on exhibit in San Francisco. Aghast that the captain treated the Lone Woman as an object- and not a person- swiftly declined. He viewed the Lone Woman as part of his family and would not sell her into slavery.

Although he turned down the captain of the Fremont's offer, there would be more offers; and each time Nidever- including Mrs. Nidever- refused. Now a member of the Nidever household, the Lone Woman decided to get to know the animals on the ranch.

> *"She takes great delight in looking at horses and cows, having probably never seen such large animals before. On one occasion she caught hold of a horse by the tail, and had it not been that Mrs. Niedever called her away, she might probably have suffered severely for her ignorance."*

But what made the Lone Woman feel right at home was spending time with Nidever's children. She even grew to love the captain's younger children as if they were her own. Every day, she watched over them, played with them for hours, showed them simple survival tricks, and told them stories- through signs and reenactments- of her adventures on the island.

As the weeks went by, the Lone Woman quickly adapted herself to the strange customs of the new people she grew to live with daily. Each day, she visited other ranchos and conversed with the women- though they didn't understand her language and went along with her symbolic gestures- and from time to time, sang and danced with them. She became the life at the party!

> *"In those days the Panama steamers used to touch at Santa Barbara, and all the passengers were desirous of seeing the lost woman. She would often put on her finest dress of feathers and go through some movements which the people termed dancing, though it had little resemblance to graceful movements of a ballroom."*

But to the small community, she became a favorite member. "She is very fond of shellfish, coffee, and liquor of every sort; but does not care for beef, pork, bread, and tea. In person she is by far the best looking Indian that I have ever seen on the coast." Repaying for her kindness, visitors would stop by the Nidever rancho and present her with gifts.

Although she accepted them, the Lone Woman did not care much for the gifts. *"She was received with the utmost kindness. Almost everyone made her a present of money clothing, or trinkets, which, however, she would immediately give to her friends, or to the children who came to see her."* Each time the visitors left, she called the children over and distributed the gifts amongst them; finding the children's happiness and joy of opening the gifts made her feel right at home- and reminding her of her deceased son. Overtime, the Lone Woman learned a few Spanish words like *papas* (potatoes), *pan* (bread), and *caballo* (horse). She even called Nidever *tata* (father) and Maria *nana* (mother).

Attempts To Communicate

From the moment of meeting her, to dancing with the neighbors, attempts to communicate with the Lone Woman remained mute. The only way Captain Nidever could effectively communicate with her was through sign language, symbols, or pantomime. Dittman describes in his memoir how the padres had Indians try to communicate with her but ended in failure.

*"The priests tried to find her life story, but she broke off
into gibberish nobody could understand. Had Indians
from Santa Barbara, Ventura, Santa Ines- they could
not understand. Understood some words but not right
through."*

Nidever elaborates in his memoir the frustrations of not finding
any remaining Nicoleño to communicate with the Lone Woman.

*"No, there was none of the Indians here that understood
her good; I tried to find some tribe that could talk to her
and finally got some woman that could talk a little. She
was raised on San Nicolas. She was fetched from some of
the islands."*

Many tried to locate the whereabouts of any Nicoleño in the area
that still spoke her language. They looked in Santa Barbara and
San Pedro but could not find any living Nicoleño in Santa Barbara
or San Pedro. It appeared the Lone Woman was the last remaining
member of the Nicoleño.

Death Of The Lone Woman

Although she was happy to be around people again, the Lone
Woman felt lonely. For several weeks, she patiently waited for
news of the Nicoleno whereabouts from Nidever, Dittman, and
Father Gonzales. We can only imagine her excitement when she
is taken to her people, reminiscing about days gone past, telling
stories about her time on the island, and thinking of the future.
Then the day finally came when Nidever broke the news to the
Lone Woman: none of the Nicoleño survived.

Hearing this devasting news must have felt like a gigantic rock
crushing her chest. The Lone Woman's once ecstatic and upbeat
demeanor drooped into melancholy. Knowing now her people
were long gone; the Lone Woman may have regretted her decision
to leave San Nicolas. She would rather die where she was born
than in a foreign country. After a few weeks of feeling down, the

Lone Woman became too weak to walk.

Every day, Nidever carried the Lone Woman to the porch and stayed in her favorite chair for hours watching the children play. In her depression, the Lone Woman would sing herself to sleep. Maria, witnessing the Lone Woman's depression, tried to cheer her up. Knowing her favorite meal was seal meat, Maria made a traditional Nicoleño meal of seal meat roasted in ashes. However, after taking one look, the Lone Woman laughed softly and refused to eat it; pointing out how worn out her teeth were from years of eating seal meat.

Record of Juana Maria's death October 19th, 1853

The Nidever family began to worry about the Lone Woman when her health took a turn for the worse. One morning on the porch, the Lone Woman fell off her chair and remained immobile for hours. It appeared to many she was on her last legs. Knowing that death was imminent, Maria hastily had a local padre, Father Francisco Sanchez, baptize her. As she took her final breaths, Father Sanchez baptized the Lone Woman and rechristened her with a Spanish name we know today: Juana Maria. Then, on the 19th of October 1853, Juana Maria, the last survivor of the Nicoleño culture, died. She was Fifty years old. Her death was recorded by Father Gonzalez in the *Book of Burials of Santa Barbara Mission.*

"On October 19, 1853, I gave ecclesiastical burial in

the cemetery to the remains of Juana Maria, the Indian
woman brought from San Nicolas Island, and since there
was no one who could understand her language, she was
baptized conditionally by Fr. Sanchez."

After her passing, the Lone Woman's possessions were given to
the California Academy of Sciences by the Nidever family.

"Among the articles she brought along with her from the
island, were several needles with which she sewed the bird's
skins together. These needles are beautifully made of fish
bones and show a superior degree of ingenuity. The thread
which she used was a thin fiber of the sinews of a whale."

Nidever further elaborates:

"She had also several fishing hooks made of old nails that
she probably found in some boards picked up on the shore.
These nails were well bent and sharpened and attached to
a line made of fibers of whale sinews beautifully twisted
together. She had also among her moveables a soft clayey
substance like brick, but whether she used this for dressing
the bird's skins, or for simply giving a red color to her
garments no one could well make out. She had a knife also
about an inch long, which seems to have been a piece of an
iron hoop. It is set in a wooden handle."

Even Father Gonzales received a few items- the cormorant dress
and bone needles- of the Lone Woman. Unfortunately, the Great
Quake of 1906 destroyed the Lone Woman's artifacts.

As for her beautiful teal cormorant dress, and bone needles, they
were given to the Pope as a gift by Father Gonzales, but since
1853, has gone missing. Perhaps they are still preserved within
the Vatican archives waiting for the world to see.As for her final
resting place, the Nidever family had the Lone Woman's body
buried in an unmarked grave- near Mission Santa Barbara. Today,

archaeologists have yet to discover her body. To commemorate her life story- and her place in California history- a statue of the Lone Woman stands at the intersection on State Street & Victoria Street in Santa Barbara. For now, her body lays undisturbed somewhere near Mission Santa Barbara, waiting to return to her island.

What Caused The Lone Woman's Death?

Many experts believe the causes that contributed to the Lone Woman's death were a combination of disease, dysentery, and changes in her natural diet- introducing her to corn, vegetables, and fruits after years of sustaining on less nutrient meals.

> *"She was excessively fond of fruit, which she would eat at all hazards. It produced dysentery, which, despite careful nursing and attendance, terminated fatally in about four weeks."*

Historians believe if she had the freedom to choose to live with the other Californian Indians and eat traditional Indian food, she could have lived a little longer; however, due to her age and poor diet, still would have succumbed to disease or dysentery.

CHAPTER ELEVEN

*"Now that the white men had come back, I could not think of what I would do
when I went across the sea or make picture in my mind of the white men and what
they did there or see my people who had been gone so long. Nor thinking of the
past, of the many summers and winters and springs that gone, could I see each
of them. they were all one, a tight feeling in my breast and nothing more."*

- ISLAND OF THE BLUE DOLPHINS (CHAPTER 29)

Although San Nicolas Island is closed off to tourists, experts
believe there had to be more to the Lone Woman's story. They
asked themselves this question: what happened to the Nicoleño
when they arrived in San Pedro in 1835? Traditionally, the
Nicoleño 's story tended to end with the remaining band boarding
the *Peor es Nada* and dying off at Mission San Gabriel-between
1835-1853. Researchers looked at Mexican records (1835-1850),
memoirs, letters, ledgers, oral histories, and anything that could
point them in the right direction. Then it dawned on them: if
you were an Indian in the 19th century, where would you be
taken to? The answer was staring them in the face: the church. To
historians, it made sense for the friars at Mission Santa Barbara
desired to have the remaining Nicoleño contraband taken to a
church to receive their baptism.

They began to look everywhere in San Pedro to find a church
with baptismal records dating somewhere from the fall of 1835
to the spring of 1836. After weeks of searching, they found the
records in one church: The Los Angeles Plaza Church. From their
research, historians found six Nicoleño Indians- 2 men and
six women- recorded in the Los Angeles Plaza Church registry

between 1835 and 1836: Black Hawk, Tomas Guadalupe, Juana, Maria Magdalena, Maria Luciana, and Maria Aleja. How did researchers know these six candidates were Nicoleño? They noted the six names recorded had secondary words next to their names: *Isla* (Island) or *Isleño* (Island Indian). Many conclude these six Isleños were the Nicoleño who departed from San Nicolas Island in late 1835. But if there were Nicoleño in California, then why couldn't Nidever, Dittman, or Father Gonzales find them?

Godparents And Godchild

As we know now, upon entering San Pedro, the remaining Nicoleño were whisked to the Los Angeles Plaza Church to receive their Christian baptism. For decades, historians accepted that some of the Nicoleño -after their baptism- were sent to work in Mission San Gabriel, while two females Nicoleño were married off to wealthy landowners in Los Angeles. However, the Mission system had undergone secularization by the Mexican government at that time; forcing many Indians- whose families had lived in the Missions in the late 18th century- off the land. So, there was no way the Nicoleño would have been taken to live in the mission, but instead may have ended up like their mission counterparts; who became destitute after secularization, were forced to work on wealthy ranchos, or become household servants.

Every day, Indian servants had to assist the matriarch with food preparation, cooking, cleaning, taking care of the children, and other backbreaking chores. But in an unusual case, the Nicoleño did not become servants nor field hands on ranchos, instead were placed in the hands of Mexican godparents. The role of the godparents was to form a supportive but respectful relationship with their Indian godchild.

> *"The godparents' obligation was to substitute for the parents if they should die, if necessary, provide for the godchild's keep and education, and give good advice." Since the Lone Woman was Nicoleño, the Nidever's became her godparents and treated her like family- which explains*

why she referred to Nidever and Maria as her "parents".

A deciding factor as to why Nicoleño went to live with their godparents was due to diseases. The Nicoleño, having been isolated for thousands of years, were still vulnerable to diseases-like smallpox, measles, whooping cough, etc.- that wreaked havoc on the Indian population within Los Angeles during the 1830s and 1840s. Even mainland Indians were not safe from catching diseases.

Whatever diseases the Nicoleño brought to the coastline could have decimated the mainlanders. It was in the best interest of the Nicoleño for them to be segregated from the rest of the population. This could explain the assumption historians had that the Nicoleño died off from diseases, but as researchers dug into the lives of the six, they were sad at what they discovered.

The Six Nicoleño
Though we may never know his name, *Black Hawk*-name given to him by sailors- was brought to San Pedro in 1835. Many sailors describe Black Hawk as "a muscular man, [Black Hawk] appeared to have sustained a head injury that left him mentally disabled." While living in San Pedro, Black Hawk worked on the harbor by assisting hunters and sailors with daily tasks up until 1841.

Historians have debated why Black Hawk decided to stay close to the harbor for many years and not go live with godparents. They speculate that Black Hawk could have been the husband of the Lone Woman. From their perspective, it would make sense for Black Hawk to stay close to the harbor as possible because if a rescue party had gone back to San Nicolas to pick up the Lone Woman and their son, he wanted to be there to welcome them to their new homeland.

However, this theory raises too many questions. For example, why did he not stop the Lone Woman-presumably his wife-from jumping ship? Why didn't he jump off the schooner to go after her? Was he okay leaving her and their son all alone on San

Nicolas? Although a plausible theory amongst historians, there is no conventional means to determine if Black Hawk was the Lone Woman's husband.

As to what happened to Black Hawk, according to an 1841 report, he was walking on *Dead Man's Island* when he fell off a cliff near the island shoreline and died. Black Hawk's body was recorded and entombed on the small island. However, any attempts by archaeologists to unearth his body are now lost. During the early 20th century, *Dead Man's Island* underwent dredging and washed Black Hawk's body out to sea. The second Nicoleño to arrive in San Pedro was a five-year-old named Tomas Guadalupe. There is strong contention- but mostly speculative- amongst historians that the five-year-old Tomas could be the Lone Woman's firstborn.

If we consider the traditional account that the Lone Woman jumped off the *Peor es Nada* to get back to the island to find her baby, then she left Tomas amongst other Nicoleño. From her mindset, the Lone Woman thought that the schooner would stay behind long enough for her to return with her baby, yet the schooner left in post-haste. This meant the Lone Woman had left her child in the hands of strangers. If this is true, does not mean the Lone Woman was a terrible mother. She would not leave her child temporarily if she was not going to come back, but she didn't.

There is no record of Tomas having both parents with him and being alone, yet the idea of him being related to the Lone Woman sounds plausible, yet without context, it remains a theory at best. After receiving his baptism on December 13, 1835, Tomas became the son of his new godparent Adelaida Johnson. When Tomas grew older, the family stopped treating him like their god child, but as their servant. We may never know if he enjoyed or hated being a servant.

As researchers continued scanning document after document,

they came across Tomas's name recorded in the Mexican 1844 Census. It appeared Tomas did not succumb to diseases or other natural factors. Records further elaborate what happened to Tomas: He continued being a servant to the Johnson family until 1859, when his godparents fell into financial difficulties and could no longer afford to hold on to him.

 Seeing an opportunity, Tomas gained his freedom from the Guirado family in 1859. It's interesting to note that Tomas was in the vicinity when the Lone Woman landed in Santa Barbara in 1853, but since she lived for only several weeks, there was not enough time to find him. Even if Nidever did find him, Tomas wouldn't be able to speak anap'its; and if he was related to the Lone Woman, he may have forgotten her.

 Now free, Tomas found work as a field hand for Antonio Coronel's vineyards at Alameda and Seventh streets. Tomas met and married an Indian named Refugio Lopez at the Los Angeles Plaza Church on June 11, 1860-with witnesses confirming Tomas identity. Tomas and Refugio went on to have many children. After that, the trail for Tomas grows cold, but if there are living descendants, they can be considered the last of the Nicoleño people.

 Juana was a 20-year-old Nicolena who received her baptism on March 28, 1836. According to the historical records, Juana lived with her godparents, the Guirado family. The Guiardo family happened to live close by the Johnson family. This meant Juana could have known Tomas for years. Her name even shows up alongside Tomas's in the 1844 Mexican Census. From there, her story remains sketched in mystery.

 Another Nicoleño who migrated to San Pedro was another young woman named Maria Magdalena. She received her baptism by Father Pedro Cabot on April 9th, 1836. However, her baptism was different from other Nicoleños. While the remaining five received their baptism at the Los Angeles Church Plaza, Maria was ill and received hers in a local pueblo.

Father Cabot expected Maria to recover and placed her under the care of her new godparents, Narciso Botello and Francisca Rúiz, but Maria's conditions continued to get worse. Then, on April 26th, 1836, Maria Magdalen died. Maria is the only Nicoleño we have a burial record that confirms her birthplace was indeed on San Nicolas Island:

> *"María Madalena Neophyte In the cemetery of the church of this Pueblo of Our Lady of the Angels, I gave burial to the following cadavers: ...On April 26, 1836, to María Madalena, neophyte of the islands [sic] of San Nicolas and baptized by the Reverend Father Pedro Cabot. She did not receive the last Sacraments."*

Amongst the Nicoleño to be baptized was a newborn girl named Maria Luciana. Historians believe she was born sometime during the voyage to San Pedro. She received her baptism on May 24, 1836. Whoever her parents were is not mentioned in the baptismal record. If her parents had died, they would appear as difunto (deceased). However, it is likely little Maria still had her mother.

Plaque of Juana Maria (Santa Barbara Mission)

For now, Maria, and possibly her still-living parents, became the child of her new godparents María de la Encarnación Reyes and Tomás Botiller. They had experienced taking care of other island natives on their Rancheria de Los Pimpares (*'Island Indian Village'*). As to Maria's eventual whereabouts, continue to be shrouded in mystery. Out of the six Nicoleño, Maria Aleja was the oldest. At 45, Maria was the oldest Nicoleño to have survived the trip to San Pedro. She received her baptism on July 17, 1836.

Living in San Pedro, Maria Aleja lived with her new godparent, the widow María Ignacia Amador. Amador at the time was living with her son, Ignacio Maria Alvarado, who was a close neighbor to the Johnson family, and Nieves Guirado (Juana's parents). Historians speculate that Maria Aleja could have had contact with the other Nicoleño.

The one piece that many claim could be Maria Aleja comes from the first United States census of California that shows an elderly woman living with Maria Amador- a mistake by the census taker who estimated the woman's age. As to what happened to her, is not known. She too disappeared from historical record after 1850. By the time the Lone Woman arrived in Santa Barbara in October 1853, the remaining Nicoleño were long gone, but thanks to this new evidence, she was not the last of her people. Now, their memories can continue to live on in the annals of Indian and California history.

CHAPTER TWELVE

"For a long time I stood and looked backed at the Island of the Blue Dolphins. The last thing I saw of it was the high headland. I thought of Rontu lying there beneath the stones of many colors, and of Won-a-nee, wherever she was, and the little fox that would scratch in vain at my fence, and my canoe hidden in the cave, and of all the happy days."

- ISLAND OF THE BLUE DOLPHINS (CHAPTER 29)

After the Lone Woman departed from San Nicolas in 1853, the island became a ghost of its former self, with no inhabitants save the foxes, wild dogs, mice, lizards, and birds. What remains of the Nicoleño culture were the skeletal remains of the huts, scattered tools, cave art, and the dead. As time went on, nature retook the island from its human overlord, yet hunters continued visiting San Nicolas Island to hunt otters and collect seagull eggs to their heart's content. When the international demand for royal furs died down, people began to look at San Nicolas Island as free land to colonize. Sometime after 1860, Basque herders saw San Nicolas's potential for grazing and wanted to bring their sheep from the mainland to the island; but with the wild dogs and foxes running amok on the island, the sheep would be in danger of being attacked and eaten. To solve this problem, paid hunters hunted and slaughtered all the wild foxes and dogs on the island.

Statue of the Lone Woman and Child (Mission Santa Barbara)

As the hunters slew the last wild dog, San Nicolas was free of the Nicoleño and their ancient compatriots. With the island free, the Basque herders- alongside their sheep- emigrated to San Nicolas; like the ancient Nicoleño and their canine companions had done 10,000 years ago. Because the sheep ate the short island grass at an accelerated rate, large tracts of the island became exposed to savage attacks through winds and storms. For the next several decades, the island, once a bastion of freedom for the Nicoleño, became unrecognizable; with the introduction of cattle by the 20th century. It looked like the island's history was seemingly destined to being forgotten.

Return To San Nicolas Island
In 1877, twenty-four years after the death of the Lone Woman, Hungarian emigrant Paul Schumacher, arrives in California. On the behest of the *Smithsonian Museum,* Schumacher visits and leads the first archaeological expedition of San Nicolas Island- and the Channel Islands between 1872 and 1879.

"The mortars are chiseled out of sandstone and often handsomely ornamented, some even with bas-relief, as found on San Nicolas Island; others again with shells sunk in the upper rim cemented with asphaltum. The islanders, as well as those living on the mainland, have been, no doubt, clever smokers, as pipes are not rarely found. Of works of art, sculptures were found representing sea lions, fish, fowls, and idols, etc. This work, done either in soapstone or serpentine, is neatly executed and polished."

Although Schumacher was the first person to have done archaeological work on San Nicolas, interest of the Lone Woman and the island ceased until 1939. In 1939, an archaeologist named Arthur Woodward- of the Los Angeles County Museum of Natural History- was reading up on California history when he came across the story of the Lone Woman.

He was fascinated by her incredible life journey living alone on San Nicolas Island and wanted to find the location of her huts- where Nidever and Dittman discovered her back in 1853. With both copies of Captain Nidever's and Carl Dittman's accounts, Woodward ventured out to San Nicolas Island to find the truth himself.

Using the coordinates described by Nidever and Dittman, Woodward traveled to the western end of the island. There, he not only pinpointed the correct location of the whale-bone windbreak but the remains of the whale bones- scattered across the site.

"When we reached the spot, I had indicated, there on the windswept were some nineteen pieces of whalebone, pieces of whale-bone, pieces of ribs and scapulae which were scattered on the ground in a rough circle. Since it was the only evidence of any shelter on the site which correspond to Nidever's description, it seemed logical that there could be

> *only one answer, this was the wreckage of the whale-bone*
> *and brush shelter once occupied by the lost woman of San*
> *Nicolas."*

While excavating the site, Woodward came across abandon items
that belonged Lone Woman.

> *"At Juana Maria's site…I found a chert knife blade almost*
> *inside the hut ring. We also found a number of shellfish*
> *hook blanks…a weathered bone barb for a fish harpoon*
> *a trifle N.W. of hut site…was characterized by the huge*
> *heaps of red abalone shells-pure shell with very little*
> *admixture of sand or other fixes".*

 Even though the island had been transformed by sheep grazing,
exposed to the elements, the Nicoleño's presence had not left,
but survived. Woodward became the first archaeologist to find
evidence of the Lone Woman's presence on the island 80 years
after her death. Believing he found the site of the Lone Woman's
hut, Woodward made notes of the discovery.

IMPLEMENTS FOUND ON SAN NICOLAS ISLAND.

Artifacts and bones of the Nicoleño on San Nicolas Island

The following year, Woodward returned to the site and began excavating the site of the Lone Woman's home. photographed the remaining structure, yet Woodward wanted to reconstruct the Lone Woman's windbreak. He wanted to see what the windbreak looked like when the hunting party discovered her back in the summer of 1853. With the help from his assistant, Woodwardreconstructed the hut- by standing up the whale bones- to Carl Dittman's descriptions; and went as far as recreating the moment she was discovered.

Although Woodward re-discovered the Lone Woman's windbreak at San Nicolas, any future attempt to excavate the island ended before they began. In 1940- one year before the Japanese kamikazed Pearl Harbor- the U.S. military decided to kick out the sheep farmers and renovate the island as a strategic naval base; testing rockets from the late 1950s to the mid-1970s. However, after the success of Island of the Blue Dolphins, San Nicolas became a hot bed for archaeological excavations.

New Discoveries
In the new millennium, new archaeological discoveries at San Nicolas Island helped expand the story of the Lone Woman. For example, in 2009, Dr. Jon Erlandson- a professor of Anthropology at the University of Oregon- visited San Nicolas Island to locate the remains of archaic Nicoleño campsites when he made an important discovery. While walking along the edge of a sea cliff, he noticed a whale rib sticking out from the cliffside.

At first, Erlandson was perplexed seeing a whale rib this far up the island- he thought the whalebone was an ancient fossil- but when he got closer, he discovered an opening. Within the exposed bone was a broken red box. After delicately removing the box from its ancient cradle, Erlandson saw a tiny twinkle and cautiously outstretched his hand into the box. He pulled out a piece of an old green glass bottle chipped into an arrowhead, then a brass button, finely carved soapstone beads, and animal effigy.

Erlandson knew the importance of his discovery was big and was lucky to have found the boxes when he did because a big storm was heading towards the island and would have washed into the ocean! After the storm died down, Erlandson returned to the cliffside and discovered two more red boxes and the remains of sealed Nicoleño water bottles.

From these boxes, Erlandson found over 200 artifacts: metals, abalone shell dishes, fishhooks, bird-bone pendants, red ochre, soapstone ornaments, glass tip heads, and bone harpoons- that weren't indigenous to San Nicolas but to native peoples of the Pacific Northwest up to the Aleutian Islands. These harpoons were either left behind by the Aleuts back in 1814 or possibly traded to the Nicoleño.

After careful examination, Erlandson concluded that the Nicoleño used these red boxes acted as a toolbox for the Nicoleño to store raw materials. He believed the first box he discovered could have belonged to the Lone Woman. Another archaeologist, Steve Schwartz, was inspired by the Lone Woman's story; he too wanted to find the precise spot Arthur Woodward first discovered- and photographed- the remains of her whalebone windbreak. It took some time, but Schwartz found where the whalebones once stood.

Nicoleño Red Box

To his surprise, despite exposure, earthquakes, and harsh winds, the whale bones had survived; as a testament of the Nicoleño 's strong will on the island. Then, in 2012, Schwartz discovered the cave where the Lone Woman made as her secondary home; by taking an 1879 map- where it showed the exact spot of the cave. After removing 40,000 buckets of sand, he uncovered the opening of the Lost Woman's cave.

However, after 2012, all archaeological study on the cave- and San Nicolas Island- was halted when the Pechanga Band of the Luiseno claimed their people had a close relationship with the Nicoleño. Today, San Nicolas remains a sacred site to the Luiseno. More recently, there have been incremental conservative efforts by wildlife watchers to protect the plant and wildlife of San Nicolas Island. Perhaps one day, archaeologists could return to complete their studies- while respecting the legacy of the Nicoleño - find and identify the remains of the Lone Woman in Santa Barbara and bring her home to her people.

LEGACY

"More than anything, it was the blue dolphins that took me back home."

- ISLAND OF THE BLUE DOLPHINS (CHAPTER 10)

The story of the Lone Woman and the Nicoleño is a story that reminds us of the tragedies many American Indians had to endure since Christopher Columbus's discovery of the New World in 1492. With their sovereignty tainted by ambition and greed, many Indians were unjustly massacred by foreigners- and other Indians- and forcibly removed from their ancestral homelands. Many Indians living in California had suffered greatly under the rule of the Spanish, Mexican, and Americans. They were hunted, forced to forsake their traditions, stripped of their identity, and lived as the poorest of whites on the reservations- all under the guise of teaching them a "lesson".

As time went on, tensions between Indians and whites settled, but not in Indian favor. Their children would be taken from their arms and be sent to *Sherman Indian School*- California's first boarding school- where their long jet-black hair be cut, forced to speak English, worked long grueling hours, died from diseases, loneliness, and neglect, and taught in the ways of the white man; ending generations of elders passing down knowledge and history to the next generation.

Even though California had changed hands for a third time, it appeared history repeated itself as the Indians- who once walked freely- were still being punished and not treated as equals. We must remember that the history of atrocities committed onto American Indians cannot be changed. Many would try to "force," condemn, and change the history- to suit their personal views- and in doing so, they failed to learn from these events.

Sculpture of Juana Maria (the Lone Woman)

To move forward, we must learn to accept what happened to all American Indians, correctly teach children and adults how to view history, and make sure to never repeat the same patterns in the future Despite the atrocities committed on Californian Indians, it is a surprise to many how the story of the Nicoleño have survived to the modern-day. They too were treated just as badly by foreigners and were tricked into leaving their ancestral home, and in the end lost everything, yet their story is a testimony to the resilience of the strong spirit.

We may never know what made the Nicoleño laugh, smile, be angry, upset, afraid, or excited, yet we know who they were and how they lived. If they feared being wiped out or forgotten, they could rest knowing that their lives and culture do matter; for their story is not only important to the story of California but to the history of all American Indians.

The Lone Woman never forgot her people, nor the teachings she learned as a little girl. She kept the Nicoleño culture alive so that one day she would be able to teach them to the next generation; however, in life, she taught us how, when stripped of family, community, and society, the human spirit can be resilient.

She managed to not only survive alone on San Nicolas Island for 18 years but thrived. By all accounts, the life of the Lone Woman contributed a renewed interest to a part of California history ignored-in favor of the Mission system and the *Gold Rush*-or forgotten by historians, teachers, and Californians by those who grew up loving *Island of the Blue Dolphins;* who sought out the truth of the Lone Woman were the difference makers in the end. Thanks to their passion for history and the Lone Woman's story, we are once again connected to the Nicoleño. Hopefully one day, the Lone Woman and the Nicoleño will become more recognizable amongst Californians- and taught in school as part of the curriculum- and children, but for now, their voices are here to stay.

TIMELINE

"There wa a legend among our people that the island had once been covered with tall trees. This was a long time ago, at the beginning of the world when Tumaiyowit and Mukat ruled. The two gods quarreled about many things. Tumaiyowit wished people to die. Mukat did not. Tumaiyowit angrily went down, down to another world under this world, taking his belongings with him, so people die because he did."

- ISLAND OF THE BLUE DOLPHINS (CHAPTER 12)

15,000–18,000 BC- Ancient humans travel on the Bering Land Bridge and begin populating the interior of the Americas; ancestors of the Nicoleño settle on southern coast of California.

10,000 BC- Ancestors of the Nicoleño migrate and settle on San Nicolas Island.

7,000- 5000 BC- The Nicoleño introduces dogs and foxes to San Nicolas Island.

1519-1521 AD- Spanish Conquistador Hernán Cortés conquers the Aztec Empire.

1532-1535 AD- On an expedition for the Spanish Crown, Hernán Cortés discovers Baja California.

1542-1543 AD- Spanish explorer Juan Rodriguez Cabrillo explores the coast of California; gives San Nicolas the moniker *'Passing Island'*.

1602 AD-Spanish explorer Sebastian Vizcaino renames *Passing*

Island to *Saint Nicolas Island.*

1769 AD- Father Junipero Serra finds the first mission in California: *Mission San Diego de* Alcalá; kicking of the 21 Mission System of California

1785-1841 AD- The *California Fur Rush* Begins

1799 AD- The *Russian American Company* is founded by Tsar Paul I.

1803 AD- The Lone Woman (*Juana Maria*) is born at the height of the *California Fur Rush.*

1810-1821 AD- Mexico begins their fight for independence against Spain

1814-1815 AD- The Russians and Aleuts land on San Nicolas to hunt otter; an Aleut hunter is slain by the Nicoleño kicking off the *Nicoleño Massacre.*

1815-1835 AD- The Decline of the Nicoleño

1821 AD- Mexico gains their independence

1833 AD- The California Missions undergo Secularization

1835 AD-The *Peor es Nada* lands on San Nicolas Island to bring the Nicoleño to San Pedro; the Lone Woman, realizing her child is still on the island, jumps ship and stays behind.

1835-1853 AD- The Lone Woman lives on San Nicolas Island for 18 lonely years.

1845 AD- The Nicoleño Black Hawk dies

1846-1848 AD- The Mexican-American War; and the *Bear Flag Revolt*

1847 AD- *The Boston Daily Atlas* publishes their *Female Crusoe* article: reporting on sittings of the Lone Woman.

1848 AD- The United States defeats Mexico

1847-1850 AD: Siting's of the Lone Woman goes dark

1850 AD- California becomes the 31st state. Returning visitors from San Nicolas reports of a "ghost" on the island.

1851-1852 AD- George Nidever and Carl Dittman make two trips to San Nicolas Island to find the Lone Woman.

1853 AD- Carl Dittman- alongside George Nidever and their hunting crew- discover the Lone Woman; stay for two months getting to know her while hunting otter. The Lone Woman arrives in Santa Barbara on October 1, 1853 but dies several weeks later.

1860 AD- San Nicolas Island is transformed into a sheep ranch by Basque ranchers; and Tomas Guadalupe, the last of the Nicoleño is mentioned in the 1860 U.S. Census.

1877 AD- Archaeologist Paul Schumacher conducts the first archaeological work on San Nicolas Island

1878 AD- Carl Dittman writes "*Narrative of a Seafaring Life on the Coast of California.*" George Nidever dictates his life story to Edward F. Murray.

1880 AD- Emma Hardacre publishes "*Eighteen Years Alone*" about the Lone Woman.

1898 AD- Author O'Dell Scott (Scott O'Dell) is born

1937 AD- *The Life and Adventures of George Nidever [1802–1883]: The Life Story of a Remarkable California Pioneer Told in his Own Words, and None Wasted* is edited and published.

1939-1941 AD- Arthur Woodward, inspired by Nidever's memoir, travels to San Nicolas Island and rediscovers the remains of Lone Woman's whale-bone hut; returns a year later and rebuilds the hut using the bones and begins excavating the island. After Pearl Harbor, San Nicolas becomes a naval base for the United States Army.

1957-Present AD-San Nicolas Island becomes a site for rocket research and serves as a detachment of Naval Base of Ventura County for the United States.

1958-1960 AD- Scott O'Dell begins his research on the Lone Women for *Island of the Blue Dolphins.*

1960 AD- *Island of the Blue Dolphins* is published to a resounding success.

1960-Present AD- Historians, Indian scholars, and archaeologists reorganize the history of the Lone Woman and the Nicoleño

1964 AD- Film adaptation of Island of the Blue Dolphins starring Celia Kaye is released by Universal Studios.

2009 AD- Dr. Jon Erlandson discovers two red boxes containing Nicoleño artifacts discovered on San Nicolas Island

2012 AD- Steve Schwartz discovers the Lone Woman's cave; all excavations on San Nicolas Island ends when the Pechanga Band of the Luiseno claimed to have close relations with the Nicoleño.

2012-Present AD- The discovery of the Six Nicoleño, and new theories of the Lone Woman are proposed, and continual conservation efforts of the flora and fauna on San Nicolas Island.

BIBLIOGRAPHY

Book Sources:

Aboriginal California: Three Studies in Culture History. The University of California Archaeological Research Facility. University of California, Berkely, 1963.

Davis, L. Thomas & Williams, S. Jack. *Indians of the California Mission Frontier (People of the California Missions).* New York: PowerKids Press. 2003. Print

Doak, Robin. *Voices From Colonial America: California 1522-1850.* National Geographic Children's Books; Illustrated edition. 2006. Print.

Heizer, R.F. & Whipple, M.A. *The California Indians: A Source Book.* London: University of California Press. 1971. Print.

Jr. Josephy, M. Alvin. *500 Nations: An Illustrated History of North American Indians.* New York: Alfred A. Knope Publisher. 1994. Print

Margaret, Amy. *The Missions of California: Mission Santa Barbara.* PowerKids Press. 2000. Print

Nidever, George. *"The Life and Adventures of a California Pioneer.*

O'Dell, Scott. *Island of the Blue Dolphins*. New York: Houghton Mifflin Harcourt Publishing Company. 1960. Print

Williams, S. Jack. *The Library of Native Americans: The Tongva of California.* New York: The Rosen Publishing Group, Inc. 2003. Print

Williams, S. Jack. *The Library of Native Americans: The Chumash of California.* New York: The Rosen Publishing Group, Inc. 2002. Print

Williams, S. Jack. *The Library of Native Americans: The Luiseno of California.* New York: The Rosen Publishing Group, Inc. 2003. Print.

Internet Sources:

Biography. *"Juan Rodriguez Cabrillo."* https://www.biography.com/explorer/juan-rodriguez-cabrillo. September 1, 2015. January 2022.Web

Blakemore, Eric. *"Stranded on the Island of the Blue Dolphins: The True Story of Juana Maria."* JSTOR Daily, February 3, 2016. https:daily.jstor.org/juana-maria-blue-dolphins/ July 2021. Web

Channelislandsnps. :*December 2018 From Shore to Sea Lecture: New Discovery in the Story of the Lone Woman."* https://www.youtube.com December 14, 2018. July 2021. Video

Daily, Marla. *"The Lone Woman of San Nicolas Island: A New Hypothesis on Her Origin."* California History. Spring/Summer 1989. https://www.islapedia.com.

July 2021. Web.

"*A Female Crusoe.*" Boston Daily Atlas, January 7, 1847.
The Lone Woman Digital Archive.
https://lonewoman.ischool.illinois.edu/lonewoman.
September 2021. Web

Hudson, Travis. "*Recently Discovered Accounts
Concerning the Lone Woman of San Nicolas
Island.*" Journal of California and Great Basin
Anthropology, 1981. https://www.islapedia.com.
July 2021. Web

Im, Sohyun. "*California Fur Rush: Historical Essay.*"
Shaping San Francisco's Digital Archive, 2013.
https://www.foundsf.org. October 2021. Web

Ishak, Natasha. "*The Tragic Story of Juana Maria: The
Woman Who Inspired Island of the Blue Dolphins.*" All
That's Interesting, September 22, 2020. https://
allthatsinteresting.com/juana-maria/ July 2021. Web.

"*Juana Maria, The Lone Woman of San Nicolas Island.*"
https://www.islapedia.com July 2021. Web.

Morris, Robert. "*DESERT SAN NICOLAS AND THE
LAST NICOLEÑO: Eighteen years alone on
California's desert island, an Indian
woman outdid Robinson Crusoe.*" The Lone Woman.Digital
Archive. https://lonewoman.ischool.illinois.edu. August 2021.
Web

Morris, L. Susan. "*The Nicolenos in Los Angeles:*

*Documenting the Fate of the Lone Woman's
  People.*" Journal of California and Great Basin
  Anthropology, Vol.36, No. 1 (2016).
    https://www.islapedia.com. September 2021

"*Russian American Company.*" https://www.britannica.com/topic/
Russian-American-Comapny. February 2022. Web

"*Paul Schumacher*" https://www.islapedia.com. April 2022. Web.

Schwartz, J. Steven. "*Some Observations on the Material
  Culture of the Nicoleno.*" 2003.
    https://www.islapedia.com. July 2021. Web

"*Scott O'Dell: Author of Island of the Blue Dolphins.*"
    https://www.scottodell.com. July 2021. Web

"*Scott O'Dell.*" Psychology Today, January 1968.
    https://www.islapedia.com. February 2022

"*Arthur Woodward.*" https://www.islapedia.com. April 2022. Web.

Woodward, Arthur. "*An Indian Woman. San Nicolas, Santa Barbara
Channel in Sierra Educational News.*"
    https://www.islapedia.com. March 1931. April 2022.   Web.

Woodward, Arthur. "*Journals of Two Voyages to San Nicolas Island,
California; April 10-April 28, 1940, and November 23-December 12,
1940.*" https://www.islapedia.com. Unpublished field notes. On
file, Los Angeles County Museum of Natural
    History. April 2022. Web

"*U.S.-Russia Relations: Quest for Stability.*"

https://www.usrussiarelations.org/2/timeline/first-contact/1. February 2022. Web

Braje, Todd. "*Voices From the Field.*" Island of the Blue Dolphins, National Park Service. https://www.nps.gov August 2021. Web

Davis, Gary. "*Voices From the Field.*" Island of the Blue Dolphins, National Park Service. https://www.nps.gov/ August 2021. Web

Erlandson, Jon. "*Voices From the Field.*" Island of the Blue Dolphins, National Park Service https://www.nps.gov/ August 2021. Web

Farris, Glen. "*Voices From the Field.*" Island of the Blue Dolphins, National Park Service. https://www.nps.gov August 2021. Web

Gill, Kristina. "*Voices From the Field.*" Island of the Blue Dolphins, National Park Service. https://www.nps.gov/ August 2021. Web

Holguin, Brian. "*Voices From the Field.*" Island of the Blue Dolphins, National Park Service. https://www.nps.gov/ August 2021. Web

James, Steven. "*Voices From the Field.*" Island of the Blue Dolphins, National Park Service. https://www.nps.gov/ August 2021. Web

Lassos, Jerry. "*Voices From the Field.*" Island of the Blue Dolphins, National Park Service. https://www.nps.gov August 2021. Web

Morris, Don. "*Voices From the Field.*" Island of the Blue Dolphins, National Park Service. https://www.nps.gov/ August 2021. Web

Morris, Susan. "*Voices From the Field.*" Island of the Blue Dolphins, National Park Service. https://www.nps.gov/August 2021. Web

Munro, Pamela. "*Voices From the Field.*" Island of the Blue Dolphins, National Park Service. https://www.nps.gov/ August 2021. Web

Schwartz, Stephen. "*Voices From the Field.*" Island of the Blue Dolphins, National Park Service. https://www.nps.gov/ August 2021. Web

Schwebel, Sara. "*Voices From the Field.*" Island of the Blue Dolphins, National Park Service.https://www.nps.gov/ August 2021. Web Soto-De, Ygnacio Ernesto. "*Voices From the Field.*" Island of the Blue Dolphins, National Park Service. https:// www.nps.gov/ August 2021. Web

Thomas, Lisa. "*Voices From the Field.*" Island of the Blue Dolphins, National Park Service. https://www.nps.gov/August 2021. Web

Timbrook, Jan. "*Voices From the Field.*" Island of the Blue Dolphins, National Park Service. https://www.nps.gov/ August 2021. Web

Ugoretz, John. "*Voices From the Field.*" Island of the Blue Dolphins, National Park Service.

https://www.nps.gov/ August 2021. Web

Vellanoweth, René. *"Voices From the Field."* Island of the Blue Dolphins, National Park Service. https://www.nps.gov/ August 2021. Web

Picture Sources

Babbage. *Statue of Juana Maria and Child.* Category: Images-Wikimedia Commons. https://commons.wikimedia.org >wiki>Category: Images. Created February 7, 2015. April 2022. Web

Category: Images-Wikimedia Commons. https://commons.wikimedia.org >wiki>Category: Images

Crenshaw, Jeremy. "Puffin PS268 (1966): *Island of the Blue Dolphins Film cover.* https://www.flickr.com/photos. Puffin Books. Taken April 11, 2021. April 2022. Web.

Islapedia. *O'Dell, Scott.* https://www.islapedia.com/index.php? title= O'Dell,_Scott March 2022. Web

Islapedia. *Nidever, George.* https://www.islapedia.com/index.php? title= Nidever,_George. March 2022. Web

Johnson, B. Neal. *A plaque commemorating Juana Maria at Santa Barbara Mission cemetery, placed there by the Daughters of the American Revolution 1928.* https://www.flickr.com/neal-j/365128128/ Taken July, 27, 2009. April 2022. Web.

ABOUT THE AUTHOR

Travis "T.j." Frank

TRAVIS "T.J." FRANK has always been fascinated by Island of the Blue Dolphins. As a native Californian, he not only wanted to learn more about the real-life Karana but the history of all American Indians. He has a BA in History. He has written many books including Akhenaten: Egypt's Mysterious Pharaoh, The Great Belzoni: History's Real Indiana Jones, and Secret Identity: 30 Inspiring Autistic Heroes Who Shaped History. He currently resides in California

BOOKS BY THIS AUTHOR

Akhenaten: Egypt's Mysterious Pharaoh
The Great Belzoni: History's Real Indiana Jones
Secret Identity: 30 Inspiring Autistic Heroes Who Shaped History

Made in the USA
Las Vegas, NV
07 June 2024